CONTINENTAL AFRICA 48

CONTINENTAL EUROPE 60

ULTIMATE POCKET
WORLD
ATLAS

A DORLING KINDERSLEY BOOK

PROJECT CARTOGRAPHY AND DESIGN
Julia Lunn   Peter Winfield

CARTOGRAPHIC RESEARCH
Michael Martin

PROJECT EDITOR AND INDEX-GAZETTEER
Jayne Parsons

DIGITAL BASE MAPS PRODUCED ON DK CARTOPIA BY
Simon Lewis   Rob Stokes   Thomas Robertshaw

PRODUCTION CONTROLLER
Hilary Stephens

EDITORIAL DIRECTOR
Andrew Heritage

ART DIRECTOR
Chez Picthall

Produced by Dorling Kindersley Cartography

First published in Canada in 1996
by élan press,
an imprint of General Publishing Co. Ltd.,
30 Lesmill Road, Toronto, Canada, M3B 2T6

Canadian Cataloguing in Publication Data
Ultimate Pocket World Atlas

ISBN: 1-55144-122-5

1. Atlases, Canadian.

G1021.057 1996   912   C95-933271-5

Film output in England, by Euroscan
Printed and bound in Italy, by L.E.G.O.

ULTIMATE POCKET
WORLD
ATLAS

élan press

KEY

—	International border
= =	Disputed border
- -	Claimed border
~	International border along river
⏤	State border
~	State border along river
~	River
~	Lake
~	Canal
~	Seasonal river
~	Seasonal lake
⤙	Waterfall
—	Road
—	Railway
●	Capital city
◎	Major town
○	Minor town
●	Major port
●	Minor port
✈	International airport
▲	Spot height – feet
•	Spot depth – feet

CONTENTS

THE PHYSICAL WORLD

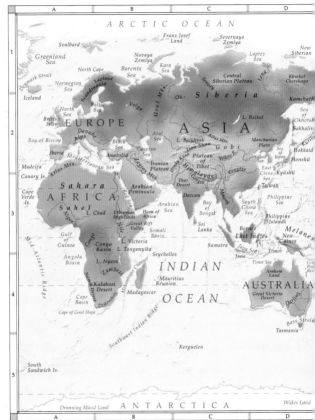

THE POLITICAL WORLD

For full list of abbreviations see page 134.

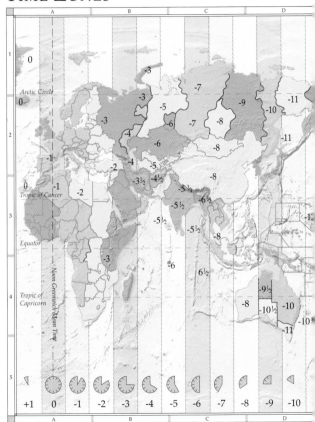

Numbers on the map indicate the number of hours which must be added or subtracted, as appropriate, in that time zone to reach GMT.

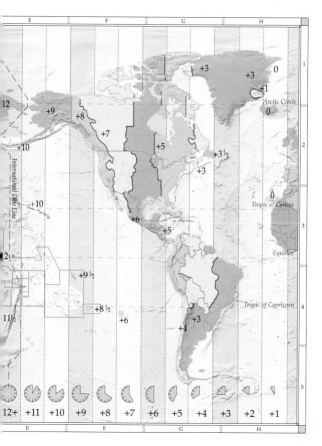

THE ARCTIC OCEAN

ASIA

ARCTIC OCEAN

NORTH AMERICA

Laptev Sea

East Siberian Sea

Chukchi Sea

Beaufort Sea

Bering Strait

Arctic Circle

Limit of permanent pack ice

Tiksi

Lena

Pevek

Wrangel I.
(Russ. Fed.)

New Siberian Is.
(Russ. Fed.)

Severnaya Zemlya

Lomonosov (Harris) Ridge

Fram (Amundsen) Basin

Canada
(Laurentian) Basin

Mackenzie

Tuktoyaktuk

Banks I.
(Canada)

Prince Patrick I.
(Canada)

Melville I.
(Canada)

Bathurst I.
(Canada)

Queen Elizabeth Is.
(Canada)

von Roberts

92

92

92

14

E

D

C

B

A

1   2   3   4

0 km   500

0 miles   500

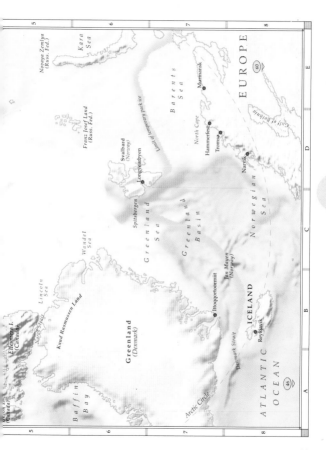

CONTINENTAL NORTH AMERICA

ARCTIC OCEAN

Limit of permanent pack-ice

Chukchi Sea

Beaufort Sea

9,059ft

Brooks Range

Melville I.

Viscount Melville Sound

Banks I.

Amundsen Gulf

Victoria I

Arctic Circle

ASIA

Bering Strait

St Lawrence I.

USA (Alaska)

Yukon

Denali 20,333ft

Alaska Range

Mt. Logan 19,850ft

Mackenzie

Great Bear Lake

Great Slave Lake

Nunivak I.

Bering Sea

Alaska Peninsula

Kodiak I.

Queen Charlotte Is.

Rocky Mountains

C A N

Aleutian Islands

Queen Charlotte Sound

Aleutian Trench

Gulf of Alaska

Vancouver I.

Mt. Rainier 14,410ft

Mt. St Helens 8,366ft

Coast Ranges

Cascade Range

Black Hills

Great Basin

Great Salt Lake

Death Valley -282ft

Mt. Whitney 14,492ft

Colorado Plateau

Sonoran Desert

Sierra Madre

Grande

PACIFIC OCEAN

Tropic of Cancer

USA (Hawaiian Is.)

Baja California

Sierra Madre Occidental

Colin 14,20

14

0 km   1000

0 miles   1000

WESTERN CANADA & ALASKA

RUSSIAN
FEDERATION

Wrangel I.

ARC

OCE

Bering Strait

Arctic Circle

Attu I.

*Bering
Sea*

St. Lawrence I.

Kiska I.

Prudh
Bay

Brooks Range

Nunivak I.

ALASKA
(USA)

Yukon

Aleutian Islands

Fairbanks

Umnak I.
Dutch Harbor○
Unalaska I.

Alaska Range

Anchorage○

Daws

Kodiak I. ○Kodiak

Valdez○

Cordova○

YUKON
TERRITO

WHITEHORSE○

Aleutian Trench

*Gulf
of
Alaska*

JUNEAU○

PACIFIC

Ketchikan○

OCEAN

Prince Rupert○

Queen Charlotte Is.

*Queen Charlotte
Sound*

Port Alice○

Vancouver I.

VICTOR

60°

180°

180°

140°

0 km   400

0 miles   400

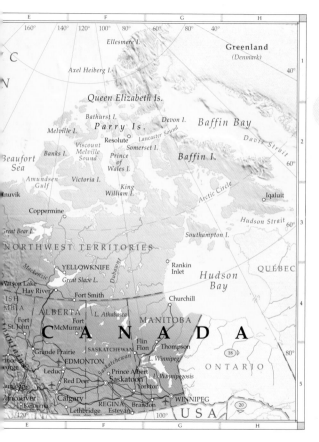

EASTERN CANADA

0 km   400

0 miles   400

E   F   G   H

70°   60°   60°

Baffin I.

Labrador
Sea

⌖12

Hudson Strait

Akpatok I.
(NW Territories)

C. Chidley

Labrador Basin

1

⌖46

Ungava
Bay

ATLANTIC

Kuujjuaq   Nain

OCEAN

Scheffervillle

Hopedale
Makkovik

Cartwright

2

Labrador

Port Hope Simpson

Caniapiscau

Smallwood
Reservoir

Churchill Falls

Happy Valley-
Goose Bay

Strait of Belle Isle

Réservoir
Caniapiscau

Labrador City

NEWFOUNDLAND

50°

D

A

Newfoundland

3

E

Réservoir
Manicouagan

Havre-
Saint-Pierre

Gander

Grand Falls

Clarenville

C

Sept-Îles

Île d'Anticosti

Corner Brook

ST JOHN'S

L. Saint-Jean

Gulf of St.Lawrence

Channel-Port-aux-Basques

C. Race

Jonquière

Gaspé

St Pierre

Chicoutimi

St. Lawrence

Bathurst

PRINCE
EDWARD
ISLAND

St Pierre & Miquelon
(France)

Grand Banks

4

QUÉBEC

NEW
BRUNSWICK

CHARLOTTETOWN

Sydney

NOVA SCOTIA

FREDERICTON

Moncton

Trois-Rivières

MAINE

Sherbrooke

20

Saint John

Dartmouth

HALIFAX

ontreal

Sohm Plain

NEW
HAMPSHIRE

Yarmouth

C. Sable

VERMONT

MASSACHUSETTS

ATLANTIC

RHODE ISLAND

CONNECTICUT   70°

OCEAN

60°

E   F   G

USA: The Northeast

0 km   200

0 miles   200

USA: CENTRAL STATES

0 km   200

0 miles   200

23

USA: THE WEST

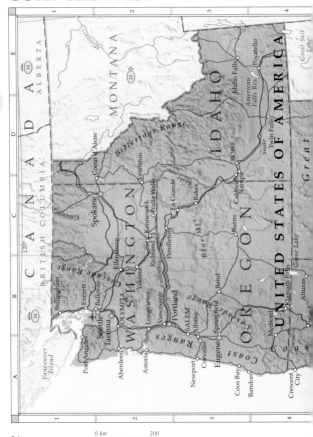

0 km 200

0 miles 200

USA: The Southwest

0 km   200

0 miles   200

USA: THE SOUTHEAST

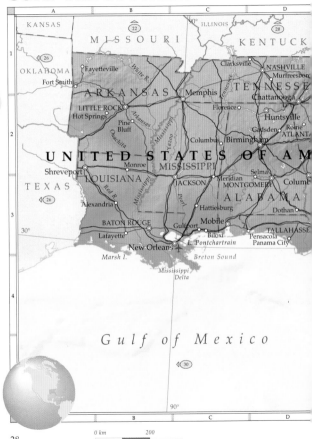

0 km   200

0 miles   200

MEXICO

0 km   200

0 miles   200

CENTRAL AMERICA

MEXICO

GUATEMALA

BELIZE

Belize City
BELMOPAN
Flores
San Ignacio

Islas de la Bahía

Gulf of Honduras

Huehuetenango
Cobán
Lago
de Izabal
Puerto
Barrios
Puerto Cortés
La Ceiba
Trujillo

Quezaltenango
Zacapa
San Pedro
Sula

GUATEMALA
CITY
Santa Rosa
de Copán
Comayagua
HONDURAS
Juticalpa

Mazatenango
La Esperanza
TEGUCIGALPA
Escuintla

Santa Ana
San Miguel
San Lorenzo

SAN SALVADOR
Choluteca
Somoto
Jinotega

EL SALVADOR
Estelí
Matagalpa

Chichigalpa
Corinto
León

MANAGUA
Juigalpa

Granada
Lago de
Nicaragua

Rivas

NICARAGUA

Middle America Trench

Gulf of Fonseca

PACIFIC

Península de
Nicoya
Liberia

OCEAN
Puntarenas
Alajue
SAN JOS

Golfo de Nicoya

90°

10°

Patuc
Co

90°

0 km   200

0 miles   200

THE CARIBBEAN

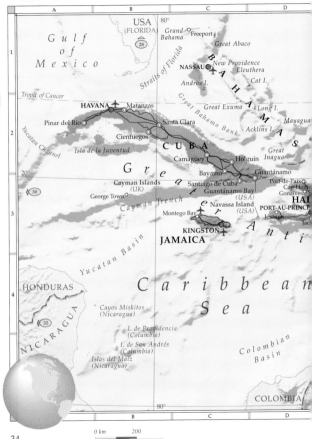

A   B   C   D

USA
(FLORIDA)

Gulf

of

Mexico

80°

Grand ○ ○ Freeport
Bahama

Great Abaco

New Providence
NASSAU ○ Eleuthera

Andros I.

Cat I.

Straits of Florida

Tropic of Cancer

HAVANA ✈ ● Matanzas

Pinar del Rio ○

Santa Clara
○

Cienfuegos ○

CUBA

Great Exuma   Long I.

Great Bahama Bank

Mayagua

Acklins I.

Camagüey ○   ○ Holguín

Yucatan Channel

Isla de la Juventud

Greater

20°

Cayman Islands
(UK)

George Town ○

Bayamo ○

Santiago de Cuba ○

Guantánamo Bay
(USA)

○ Guantánamo

Great
Inagua

Port-de-Paix ○
Cap-Haïti

Gonaïve

Cayman Trench

Navassa Island
(USA)

Montego Bay ○

Jérémie ○

HAI

PORT-AU-PRINCE ✈

Jac

KINGSTON

JAMAICA

A

n

t

i

HONDURAS

Yucatan Basin

C a r i b b e a n

S e a

Cayos Miskitos
(Nicaragua)

NICARAGUA

I. de Providencia
(Columbia)

I. de San Andrés
(Columbia)

Islas del Maíz
(Nicaragua)

Colombian

Basin

COLOMBIA

80°

B   C   D

0 km   200

0 miles   200

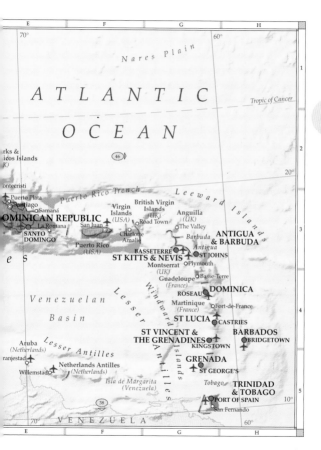

CONTINENTAL SOUTH AMERICA

0 km 1000

0 miles 1000

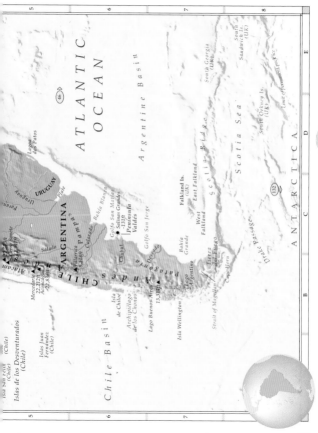

ATLANTIC OCEAN

Argentine Basin

Scotia Ridge

South Georgia (UK)

South Sandwich Is. (UK)

Scotia Sea

South Orkney Is. (UK)

Limit of Permanent Ice Pack

ANTARCTICA

Lagoa dos Patos

URUGUAY

Río de la Plata

Paraná

ARGENTINA

Pampas

Colorado

Bahía Blanca

Salinas Grandes -131ft

Península Valdés

Golfo San Matías

Chubut

Golfo San Jorge

CHILE

Salado

Mercedario 22,211ft
Aconcagua 22,831ft

Cerro Bonete 22,175ft

Atacama

Andes

Patagonia

Falkland Is. (UK)

West Falkland

East Falkland

Bahía Grande

Deseado

Lago Argentino 13,159ft

Isla de Chiloé

Archipiélago de los Chonos

Lago Buenos Aires

Isla Wellington

Tierra del Fuego

Strait of Magellan

Cape Horn

Drake Passage

Chile Basin

Isla San Félix (Chile)

Islas de los Desventurados (Chile)

Islas Juan Fernández (Chile)

NORTHERN SOUTH AMERICA

Antilles
GRENADA
60°
46

Isla de Margarita
Carúpano   TRINIDAD
Cumaná   & TOBAGO
Maiquetía   1   10°
Barcelona
El Tigre   Maturín
Tucupita   A T L A N T I C
n   o   s
Orinoco   Ciudad Guayana   Morawhanna
Ciudad Bolívar   O C E A N
Embalse
de Guri

ZUELA   Cuyuni   2
GEORGETOWN   Nieuw
Bartica   New Amsterdam Amsterdam
Rockstone   Linden PARAMARIBO St.-Laurent-
GUYANA   du-Maroni
Guiana   Sinnamary
Highlands   W.J. van   Kourou
Blommesteinmeer
Kabalebo   Cayenne
Reservoir
Orinoco   SURINAME   French
Guiana
(France)   3
Essequibo
Acarai Mts.   Corentijn
Courantyne

Equator 0°

B   R   A   Z   I   L   4

Amazon
40

60°

E   F   G   H

39

Peru, Bolivia & North Brazil

PARAGUAY, URUGUAY & SOUTH BRAZI

0 km   200

0 miles   200

Uberlândia
40
ZIL
Uberaba
Rio Grande
Belo Horizonte
Governador
Valadares
Abrolhos
Bank
Hotspur
Seamount
Franca
Divinópolis
Represa de Furnas
Ribeirão Preto
Vitória
Champlaim
Seamount
20°
Montague
Seamount
Juiz de Fora
Cachoeiro de
Itapemirim
Vitória
Seamount
Jaseur
Seamount
Volta Redonda
Campinas
Nova Iguaçu
Campos
Sorocaba
Taubaté
São Paulo
Rio de Janeiro
Santos

Tropic of Capricorn

Santos
Plateau

ATLANTIC

OCEAN

46

30°

Rio
Grande
Rise

Argentine
Basin

40°

CHILE & ARGENTINA

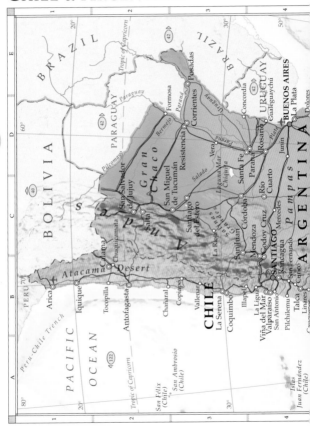

0 km   200

0 miles   200

44

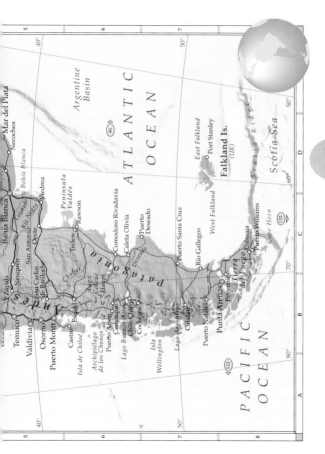

Mar del Plata
Necochea

Argentine
Basin

A T L A N T I C

O C E A N

Bahía Blanca
Bahía Blanca
San Antonio Oeste
Viedma

Colorado
Río Negro

Peninsula
Valdés

Rawson

East Falkland
Port Stanley

Falkland Is.
(UK)

Scotia Ridge

Scotia Sea

Neuquén
Za Zapala

San Carlos
de Bariloche

Trelew
Comodoro Rivadavia
Caleta Olivia
Puerto Deseado
Puerto Santa Cruz

West Falkland

Chubut

Lago
Colhué
Huapi

Deseado

P a t a g o n i a

Río Gallegos

Cabo Horn

Puerto Williams

Andes

Temuco
Valdivia
Osorno
Puerto Montt

Castro

Isla de Chiloé

Archipiélago
de los Chonos

Puerto Aisén
Coihaique
Esquel

Lago
General
Carrera

Lago Buenos Aires
Chile Chico

Cochrane

Isla
Wellington

Calafate
Puerto Natales

Lago
Argentino

Porvenir
Punta Arenas

Tierra
del Fuego

Ushuaia

P A C I F I C

O C E A N

45

THE ATLANTIC OCEAN

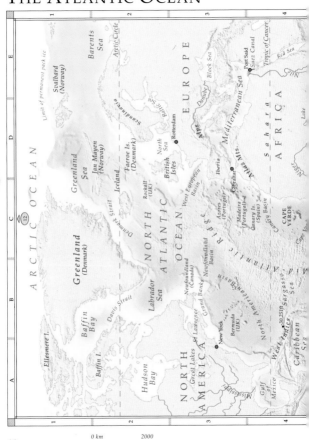

ARCTIC OCEAN

Barents Sea

Arctic Circle

Svalbard (Norway)

Limit of permanent pack ice

Jan Mayen (Norway)

Greenland Sea

EUROPE

Scandinavia

Baltic Sea

North Sea

Black Sea

Danube

Port Said

Red Sea

Suez Canal

Tropic of Cancer

Greenland (Denmark)

Denmark Strait

Iceland

Faeroe Is. (Denmark)

British Isles

Rockall (UK)

West European Basin

Alps

Mediterranean Sea

Atlas Mts.

Gibraltar

Iberia

S a h a r a

AFRICA

Nile

Lake

Ellesmere I.

Baffin Bay

Baffin I.

Davis Strait

Labrador Sea

NORTH ATLANTIC OCEAN

Newfoundland (Canada)

Newfoundland Basin

Azores (Portugal)

Madeira (Portugal)

Canary Is. (Spain)

CAPE VERDE

Canary Basin

Mid-Atlantic Ridge

Cape Ve

Grand Banks

St. Lawrence

Great Lakes

New York

Bermuda (UK)

North American Basin

30.25ft

Sargasso Sea

West Indies

Hudson Bay

NORTH AMERICA

Mississippi

Gulf Mexico

Caribbean Sea

ARCTIC OCEAN

12

0 km   2000

0 miles   2000

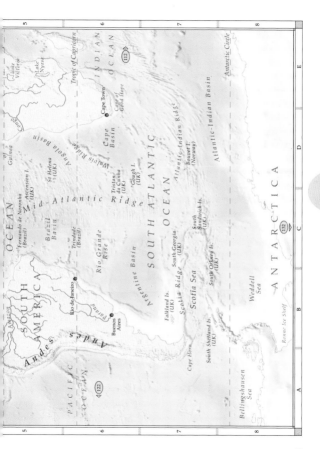

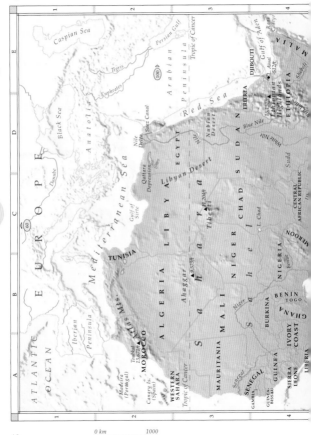

0 km 1000

0 miles 1000

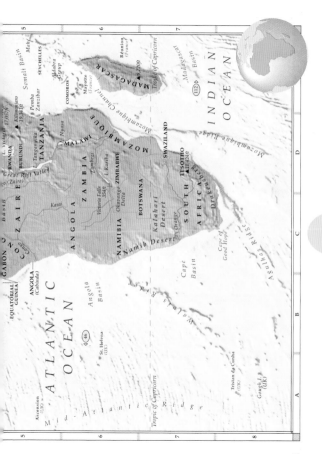

0 km   400

0 miles   400

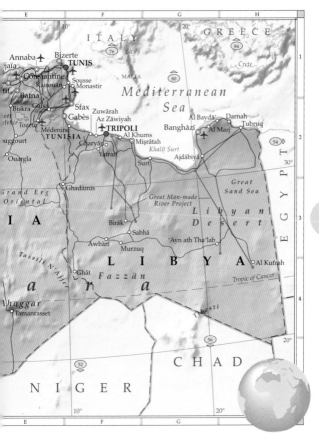

0 km   250

0 miles   250

0 km   400

0 miles   400

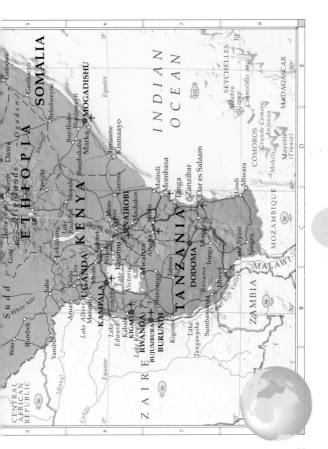

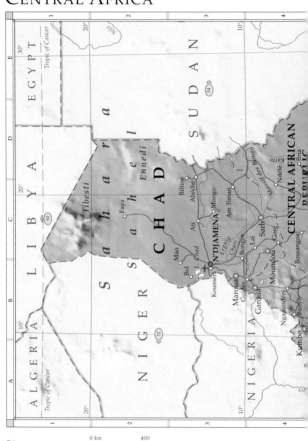

0 km   400

0 miles   400

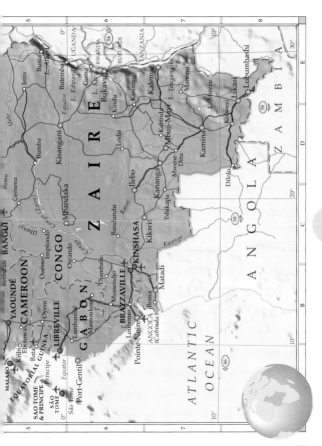

57

SOUTHERN AFRICA

0 km   400

0 miles   400

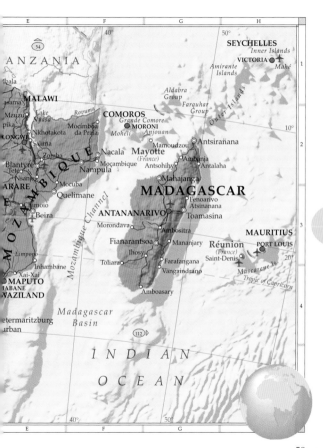

CONTINENTAL EUROPE

ARCTIC OCEAN

Norwegian Basin

Arctic Circle

Norwegian Sea

ICELAND

Faeroe-Iceland Ridge

Faeroe Islands (Denmark)

Shetland Is.

8,101ft▲ NORWAY

Kjølen Mts.

Orkney Is.

North Sea

SWEDE

Outer Hebrides

DENMARK

ATLANTIC OCEAN

UNITED KINGDOM

Elbe

IRELAND

NETHERLANDS

Thames

BELGIUM

English Channel

LUX.

GERMANY

CZE R

Danub

Seine

Rhine

Meuse

FRANCE

Loire

AUST

Biscay Plain

SWITZ. LIECH.

SLOVEN

6,188ft▲

Mt. Rh.

Bay of Biscay

Massif Central

Mont Blanc 15,772ft

ITALY SAN MARINO

C. Finisterre

Garonne

Rhône

11,168ft▲

MONACO

VATICAN CITY

Pyrenees

ANDORRA

Corsica

PORTUGAL

SPAIN

Balearic Is.

Sardinia

Tyrrhenia Sea

C. St Vincent

Guadalquivir

Mulhacen

Mediterranean Sea

Etna 11,0

Sici

Gibraltar (UK)

MALTA

AFRICA

60

0 km   600

0 miles   600

North Cape

Lapland
946ft

Barents Sea

Kola
Peninsula

White Sea

Arctic Circle

Gulf of Bothnia

FINLAND

N. Dvina

Ural Mountains

Baltic Sea

Gulf of Finland

ESTONIA

RUSSIAN FEDERATION

LATVIA

Volga

Dvina

92

LITHUANIA

USSIAN FED.
Kaliningrad)

Plain

European

BELARUS

Dnieper

uropean

Vistula

OLAND

UKRAINE

Pripet
Marshes

Carpathians

LOVAKIA

Dniester

Don

Volga

UNGARY

MOLDOVA

ROMANIA

Sea of
Azov

Volga
Delta
-92ft

Aral
Sea

OATIA
S. &
RZ.

Danube

YUGO

Balkan Mts

*Black
Sea*

Caucasus Mts.

Caspian
Sea

BULGARIA

El'brus 18,511ft

MAC.

BANIA

Pindus
Mts.

Aegean
Sea

A

S

I

A

nian
Sea

GREECE

Tigris

92

Crete

Euphrates

61

THE NORTH ATLANTIC

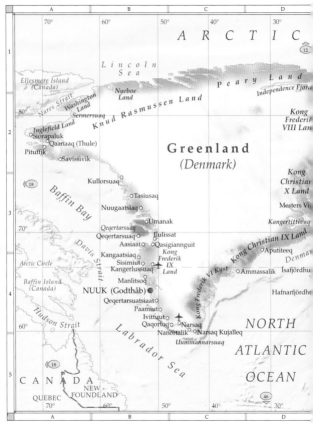

ARCTIC

Lincoln
Sea

Ellesmere Island
(Canada)

Nyeboe
Land

Peary Land

Independence Fjord

Nares Strait

Washington
Land

Sermersuaq

Knud Rasmussen Land

Kong
Frederik
VIII Land

Inglefield Land
Siorapaluk
Qaanaaq (Thule)
Pituffik
Savissivik

Greenland
(Denmark)

Kong
Christian
X Land

Kullorsuaq

Mesters Vig

Tasiusaq

Kangertittivaq

Baffin Bay

Nuugaatsiaq

Umanak

Qeqertarsuaq
Qeqertarsuaq
Aasiaat
Ilulissat
Qasigianguit

Davis Strait

Kong Frederik VI Kyst

Kong Christian IX Land

Aputiteeq

Kangaatsiaq
Kangerlussuaq

Kong
Frederik
IX
Land

Denma

Sisimiut

Arctic Circle

Ammassalik
Ísafjördhu

Manlitsoq

NUUK (Godthåb)

Hafnarfjördht

Baffin Island
(Canada)

Qeqertarsuatsiaat

Paamiut

Hudson Strait

Ivittuut
Qaqortoq
Nanortalik
Narsaq
Narsaq Kujalleq

NORTH

Labrador Sea

Uummannarsuaq

ATLANTIC

CANADA
NEW-
FOUNDLAND

OCEAN

QUEBEC

0 km   500

0 miles   500

OCEAN

Wandel Sea

Greenland Sea

Svalbard
(Norway)

Spitsbergen *Nordaustlandet*

Pyramiden

Barentsburg Longyearbyen

Edgeøya

Danmarkshavn

Daneborg

Greenland Basin

Mohns Ridge

North Cape

Jan Mayen
(Norway)

Norwegian Sea

Arctic Circle

toqqortoormiit

Húsavík

kureyri Seydhisfjördhur

REYKJAVÍK

elfoss Djúpivogur

ICELAND

Faeroe Islands
(Denmark)

Tórshavn

FINLAND

ryville-Thomson Ridge

Shetland (UK)

Orkney (UK)

NORWAY

SWEDEN

Hebrides (UK)

DENMARK

ESTONIA

LATVIA

IRELAND

UNITED KINGDOM

NETH.

GERMANY

POLAND

LITH.

SCANDINAVIA & FINLAND

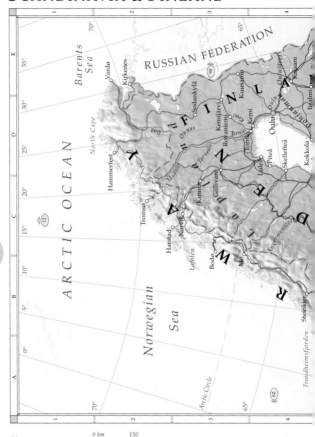

0 km 150

0 miles 150

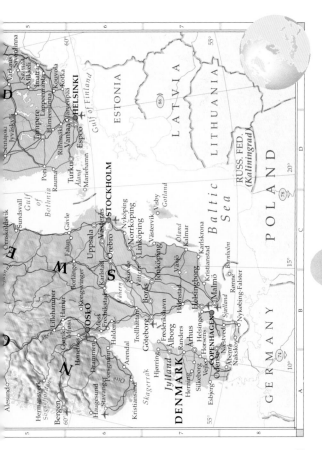

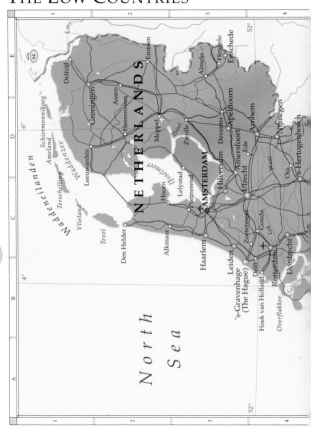

0 km   50

0 miles   50

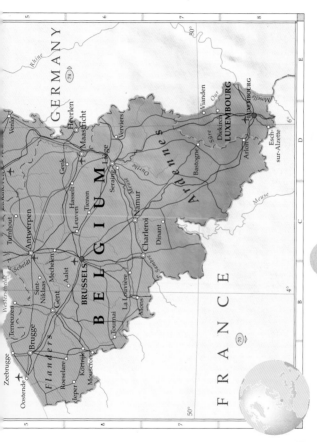

0 km   100

0 miles   100

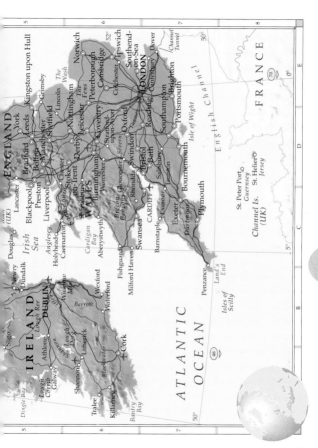

— Administrative border

FRANCE & ANDORRA

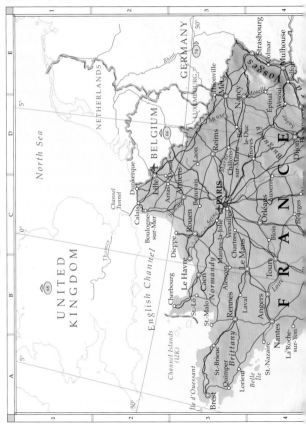

0 km   100

0 miles   100

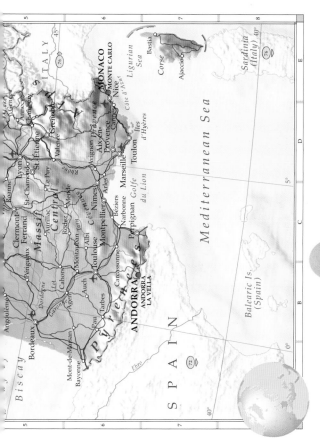

SPAIN & PORTUGAL

Bay of Biscay

F R A N C E

Pyrenees

ANDORRA

antander

Bilbao   San Sebastián

racaldo   *Basque Provinces*

iranda   Vitoria   Pamplona

le Ebro

Logroño   Huesca   Girona   Figueres

Burgos   *Costa Brava*

Soria   Lleida   *Catalonia*

Zaragoza   Terrassa   Mataró

A I N   Sabadell   Badalona

govia   Reus   Barcelona

Tarragona

MADRID   Tortosa   *Menorca*

Alcalá de Henares   Teruel

Getafe   Cuenca

ledo   Castellón   40°

de la Plana   Palma

ciudad Real   Valencia   *Mallorca*

Valencia   Gandía   *Islas Baleares*

Albacete   *Eivissa*

Linares   Elda   *Formentera*

Cieza   Benidorm

Murcia   Alicante

Lorca   Elche

Costa Blanca

Cartagena

Mediterranean Sea

ñada

a Nevada   35°

Motril   Almería

ta del Sol

0°

A L G E R I A

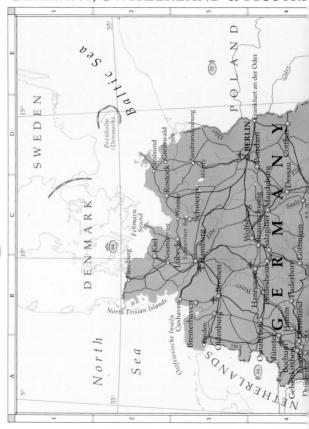

0 km   100

0 miles   100

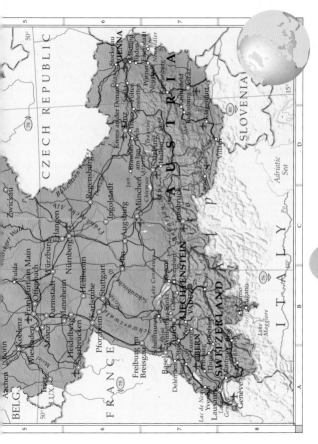

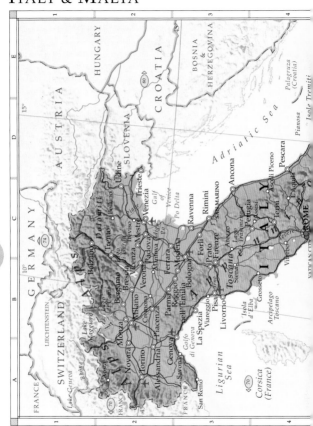

0 km   100

0 miles   100

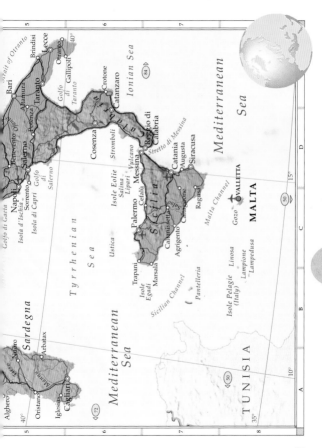

0 km   100

0 miles   100

THE WESTERN BALKANS

0 km   100

0 miles   100

THE MEDITERRANEAN

ATLANTIC

OCEAN

Thames

English Channel

Seine

Rhine

E U

Danube

46

Loire

Massif Central

Dordogne

L. Geneva

Mt. Blanc ▲

15,771ft

Alps

Po

A
l
p
s

Apennin

Genoa

Livorno

Bay of Biscay

C. Finisterre

Garonne

Ebro

Pyrenees

11,168ft ▲

Marseille

Golfe du Lion

Corsica

Iberian

Peninsula

Tagus

Valencia

Barcelona

Balearic Is.

Sardinia

Napl

Tyrrhen
Sea

M e d i t

C. St Vincent

Guadalquivir

11,168ft ▲

Gibraltar

Strait of Gibraltar

Oran

Algiers

Tell Atlas

Tunis

Me

Sfax

Rif

7,638ft ▲

A t l a s   M o u n t a i n s

Chott el Jerid

Tripoli

13,665ft ▲

46

Grand Erg Occidental

Grand Erg Oriental

Canary Is.
(Spain)

A F R I

S a h a r a

48

0 km   400

0 miles   400

BULGARIA & GREECE

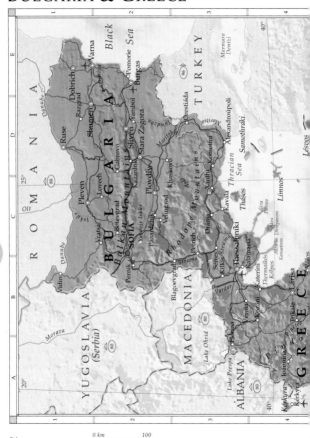

0 km 100

0 miles 100

TURKEY

96

Aegean
Sea

Chíos ○Chíos

Sámos

Ikaría

Tínos

Ándros

Mýkonos

K y k l á d e s

Kéa

Páros

Náxos

Íos

Amorgós

Astypálaia

Thíra

Dodekánisos

Kos

Ródos

Ródos

Kárpathos

35°

54

Irákleio

Sea of Crete

25°

Mýrtóo Pélagos

Mílos

Chaniá ○

Kríti

M e d i t e r r a n e a n   S e a

Léon

Chalkída
ATHENS
Achámes
Pórtoas
Dírfiga
Karínthon

Lévídia

Korinthiakós Kólpos

Korínthos

Ágrinio

○Ítáma

○Lévídia

P e l o p ó n n i s o s

Trípoli

Spárti

Kalamáta

Kýthira

Kefallinía

Zákynthos

*I o n i a n
Sea*

76

ónioi Nísoi

LIBYA

50

35°

20°

85

THE BALTIC STATES & BELARUS

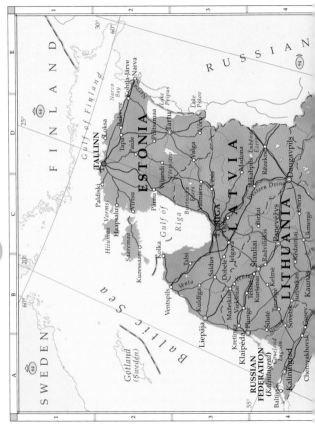

0 km 100

0 miles 100

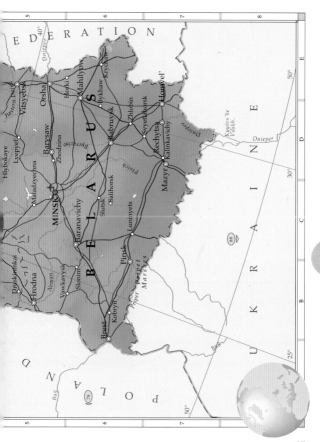

UKRAINE, MOLDOVA & ROMANIA

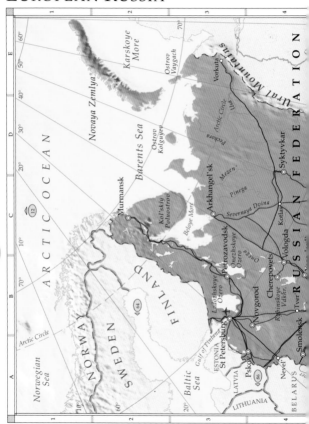

0 km   400

0 miles   400

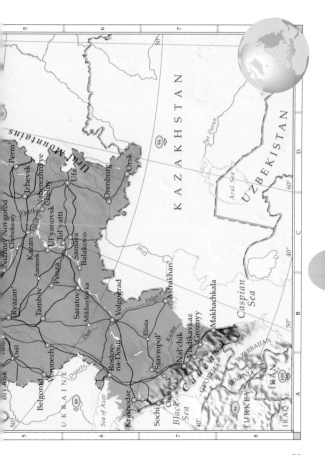

CONTINENTAL NORTH & WEST ASIA

0 km   1000

0 miles   1000

ARCTIC OCEAN

rnaya Zemlya

Laptev
Sea

New Siberian
Islands

Limit of permanent pack-ice

ymyr
ninsula

East Siberian Sea

Wrangel I.

ral Siberian
Plateau

Chukchi
Sea

e r i a

Verkhoyansk Range

Chersky Range

Arctic Circle

Lena

Kolyma Range

Bering Strait

E R A T I O N

Stanovoy Range

Dzhugdzhur Range

Sea
of
Okhotsk

Kamchatka
4750m

Bering
Sea

L. Baikal

Amur

Sakhalin

Aleutian Islands
(USA)

ng River

Sikhote-Alin Range

Sea
of
Japan

Hokkaidō

Honshū

PACIFIC
OCEAN

Yangtze

Kyūshū

Hainan
Dao

Taiwan

Northern
Marianas
(USA)

Mariana Trench

Hawaiian Is.
(USA)

Tropic of Cancer

South
China
Sea

Luzon

Guam
(USA)

Mekong

RUSSIA & KAZAKHSTAN

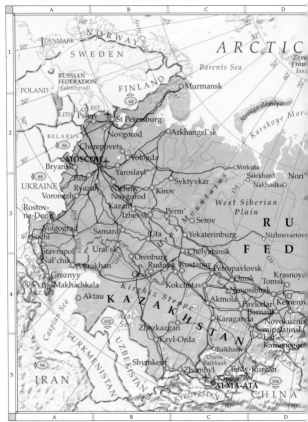

Map labels (west to east, north to south):

ARCTIC — Barents Sea — Zemlja Fran Ios — Novaja Zemlja — Karskoye Mor

NORWAY — Arctic Circle — DENMARK — SWEDEN — FINLAND — Murmansk

RUSSIAN FEDERATION (Kaliningrad) — POLAND — LAT. EST. — LITH. — Pskov — St Petersburg — Novgorod — BELARUS — Cherepovets — Vologda — MOSCOW — Vorkuta — Salekhard — Nakhodka O — Nori

Bryansk — Tula — Yaroslavl' — Arkhangel'sk — Syktyvkar — Mountains — Ob' — West Siberian Plain — R U

UKRAINE — Ryazan' — Nizhniy Novgorod — Kirov — Perm' — Serov — Yekaterinburg — Nizhnevartovs — F E D

Voronezh — Rostov-na-Donu — Izhevsk — Kazan' — Ufa — Chelyabinsk

Volgograd — Samara — Orenburg — Rudnyy — Kustanay — Petropavlovsk — Omsk — Tomsk — Krasnoya

Sochi — Stavropol' — Ural'sk — Orsk — Kokchetav — Akmola — Novosibirsk — Kemero

Nal'chik — Astrakhan' — Kirghiz Steppe — Pavlodar — Barnaul

Grozny — Makhachkala — Aktau — K A Z A K H S T A N — Karaganda — Novokuzne — Semipalatinsk — Ust-Kamenogor

GEORGIA — ARM. — AZ. — Caspian Sea — Aral Sea — Zhezkazgan — Kzyl-Orda — Balkhash — Ozero Balkhash — Taldy-Kurgan

IRAN — TURKMENISTAN — UZBEKISTAN — Shymkent — Zhambyl — Kapchagay — ALMA-ATA — CHINA — KYRGYZSTAN

0 km 500
0 miles 500

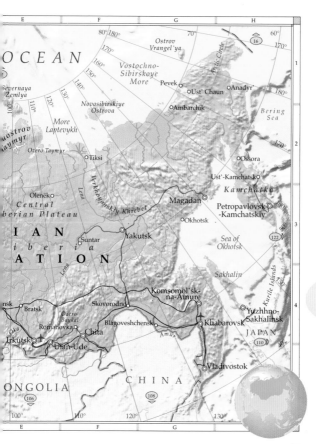

TURKEY, CYPRUS & THE CAUCASUS

0 km   200

0 miles   200

▪▪▪ *Cyprus - 1974 ceasefire line*

THE NEAR EAST

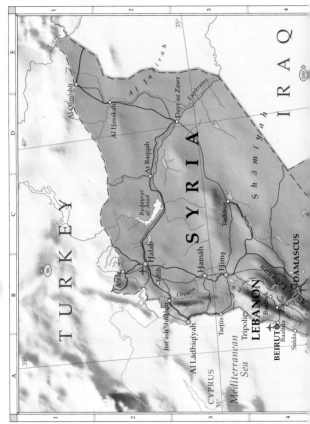

0 km   100

0 miles   100

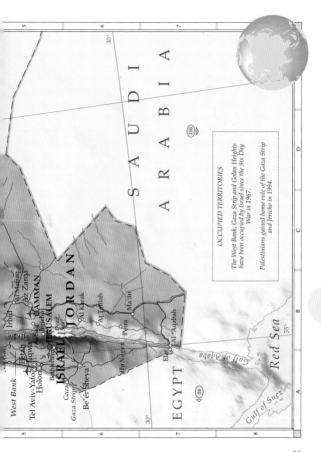

OCCUPIED TERRITORIES

The West Bank, Gaza Strip and Golan Heights have been occupied by Israel since the Six Day War in 1967.

Palestinians gained home rule of the Gaza Strip and Jericho in 1994.

THE MIDDLE EAST

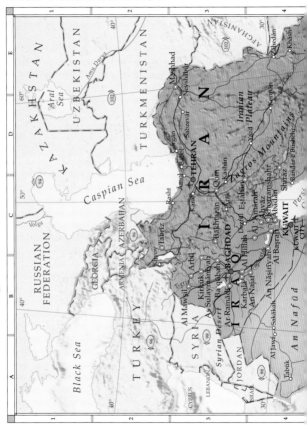

KAZAKHSTAN

Aral Sea

UZBEKISTAN

Amu Darya

TURKMENISTAN

Mashhad
Neyshābūr
Gorgān
Bābol
Sabzevār
Amol
TEHRAN
Karaj
Qom
Kāshān
Iranian Plateau

Rasht
Caspian Sea

RUSSIAN FEDERATION

Volga

GEORGIA

ARMENIA AZERBAIJAN

TURKEY

Black Sea

Khvoy
Tabrīz
Bākhtarān
I R A N
Eşfahān
Dezfūl
Yazd Plateau
Zagros Mountains
Kermān

Arbīl
Kirkūk
As Sulaymānīyah
BAGHDAD
Ar Ramādī Ba'qūbah
Al Fallūjah
Karbalā'
An Najaf
An Nāşirīyah
Al Başrah
ʻAmmārah
Khorramshahr
Ābādān
KUWAIT
KUWAIT CITY

Al Mawşil
I R A Q
SYRIA
Syrian Desert

Tigris

JORDAN
LEBANON
CYPRUS

Al Jawf
Sakākah
An Nafūd
Tabūk

KARAK

Shīrāz

Bandar-e Büshehr

AFGHANISTAN

Kāshān

0 km   400

0 miles   400

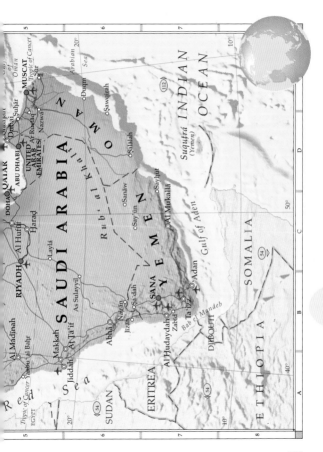

CENTRAL ASIA

KAZAKHSTAN

Aral Sea

Su-Darya

Ustyurt Plateau

UZBEKISTAN

Caspian

Zaliv Kara-Bogaz-Gol

Nukus

Keneurgench   Tel'mansk

Dashkhovuz   Urgench   Uchkuduk

Turkmenbashy   Turtkul'   Zarafsha

TURKMENISTAN   *Ozero Aydark*

Cheleken   *Kara*   *Turan   Lowland*

Nebitdag   Bukhara   Nav

Gazandzhyk   Seydi   Samarka

Sea   Chardzhev   Karshi

Gyzylarbat   *Amu Darya*   Komsomol'sk

Bakherden   Sayat   Kerki

Gekdepe   Mary   Bayramaly

Byuzmeyin   **ASHGABAT**   *Karakumskiy Kanal*

Kaka   Tedzhen   Yeloten

Tedzhen   *Murgab*

Aqchah

Sheberghan   **Mazar-e Sha**

Meymaneh

Bālā Morghāb   *Bande Torkestan*

Gushgy   *Morghāb*

Qal'eh-ye Now

I   R   A   N   Herāt   *Harīrūd*

(100)

AFGHANISTA

Farāh

Gereshk

Zaranj   Kandahar

Dasht-e Margow

Helmand

0 km   200

0 miles   200

Lake Balkhash

70°   80°

AZAKHSTAN   1

Kara-Balta **BISHKEK** Tyup
                Tokmak
Talas   Issyk-Kul'   Karakol
KYRGYZSTAN   Ozero Issyk-Kul'

HKENT Chirchik   Naryn   40°
  Angren   Narym   Naryn
Almalyk Andizhan   Dzhalal-Abad
hudzhand Kokand Osh
Tyube Sulyukta Fergana
 Zeravshan Isarkhob Khaydarkan

USHANBE **TAJIKISTAN**   C H I N A

  Dangara   Murgab   3
  Kulyab Vartang
 Parkhar Khorog
ngan- Feyzabad   Pamirs
nez Panj   Aksai Chin
olm   Kunduz Indus   Occupied by China,
                      claimed by India
  Baghlan
honvi
arikar Asadabad   4
BUL Jalalabad   Jammu & Kashmir   Demchok/Dêmqog
                  A "line of control" was agreed   Claimed by India
Ghazni   between India and Pakistan in   and China.
  Gardez   1972

  Indus

AKISTAN I N D I A

70°

E   F   G   H

EAST & SOUTH ASIA

ASIA

Lake Baikal

Aral Sea

▲ 14,312ft
Altai Mountains

MONGOLIA

Caspian Sea

Gobi

Tien Shan
14,407ft ▲
Turpan Depression
-505ft
Takla Makan

Hindu Kush

Altun Mts.

CHINA

Iranian Plateau

24,229ft ▲

Kunlun Mts.

Great P
of Chin

Plateau of Tibet

PAKISTAN **NEPAL**

H i m a l a y a s

BHUTAN

Hong Kong

Indus

Thar Desert

Ganges Plain

Macao
(Portugal)

Tropic of Cancer

Indus Delta

Mt Everest
29,030ft ▲

Ganges

BANGLADESH

Arabian Peninsula

INDIA

Ganges Delta

MYANMAR

Hainan Dao

Godavari

Irrawaddy

Arabian Sea

D e c c a n

Western Ghats

Eastern Ghats

Bay of Bengal

THAILAND

Mekong

Salween

VIETNA

LAOS

Lakshadweep
(India)

Andaman Is.
(India)

Andaman Sea

Gulf of Thailand

Sout
Chin
Sea

MALDIVES

SRI LANKA

Nicobar Is.
(India)

CAMBOD

13,455
BRUNE

MALAYSIA

Equator

SINGAPORE

Borne

▲ 12,467ft

Sumatra

IND

Java Se

INDIAN OCEAN

Krakatau
2,667ft ▲

Java

Sund
Trench

Bali

A B C D

0 km   1000

0 miles   1000

WESTERN CHINA & MONGOLIA

0 km 400

0 miles 400

Eastern China & Korea

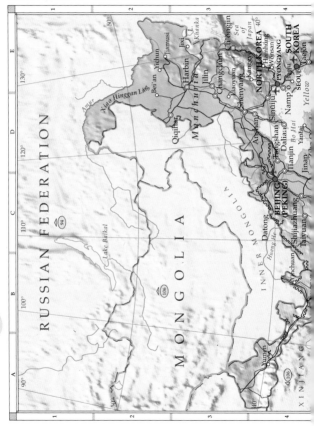

0 km 400

0 miles 400

JAPAN

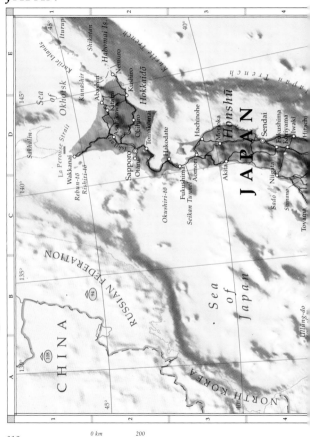

0 km 200

0 miles 200

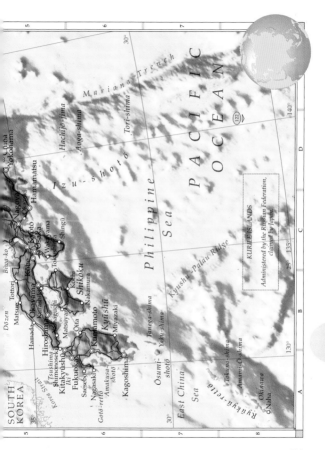

SOUTH
KOREA

Korea Strait

Dōzen

Matsue
Tottori

Hamada

Hiroshima
Tsushima
Shimonoseki
Iki
Kitakyūshū
Fukuoka
Saseho
Nagasaki
Gotō-rettō
Amakusa-shotō

Okayama
Kurashiki
Yamaguchi

Matsuyama
Ōita
Kumamoto

Miyazaki

Kagoshima

Osumi-
shotō

Biwa-ko

Kōbe
Ōsaka
Kyōto
Tsu

Wakayama

Tokushima

Kōchi

Shikoku
Nakamura

Kyūshū

Tanega-shima
Yaku-shima

Nagoya
Ōsaka
Yokohama

Hamamatsu

Shingū

Izu-shotō

Hachijō-jima
Ōkoshi

Aoga-shima

Tori-shima

Mariana Trench

30°

PACIFIC

OCEAN

Philippine

Sea

Kyushu-Palau Ridge

KURILE ISLANDS

Administered by the Russian Federation,
claimed by Japan

140°

D

135°

C

25°

130°

B

30°

A

East China

Sea

Tokuno-shima
Amami-O-shima

Okinawa
Naha

Ryūkyū-rettō

35°

5   6   7   8

THE INDIAN OCEAN

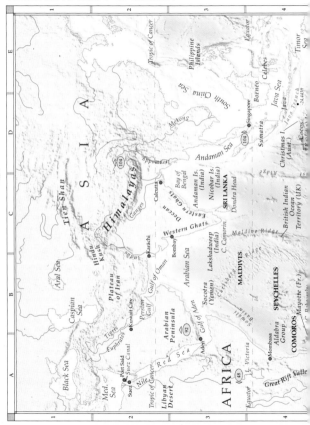

0 km 1000

0 miles 1000

AUSTRALIA
Desert
Tropic of Capricorn
Nullarbor Plain
North West C.
Fremantle
Cape Leeuwin
124

Southeast Indian Ridge

South Indian Basin

Wilkes Land

West Australia Basin

Ninety

Broken Ridge

Mid-Indian Ridge

INDIAN OCEAN

Mascarene Plateau

MAURITIUS (Fr.)

Madagascar Basin

Kerguelen (Fr.)

Heard I. (Aust.)

Kerguelen Plateau

Macdonald Is. (Aust.)

Crozet Basin

Crozet Is. (Fr.)

ANTARCTICA

Amery Ice Shelf
132

Queen Maud Land

Atlantic-Indian Basin

Madagascar Ridge

Southwest Indian Ridge

MADAGASCAR
Tropic of Capricorn
Faratangana
Prince Edward Is. (SA)
Durban
Drakensberg

113

NORTH INDIA, PAKISTAN & BANGLADESH

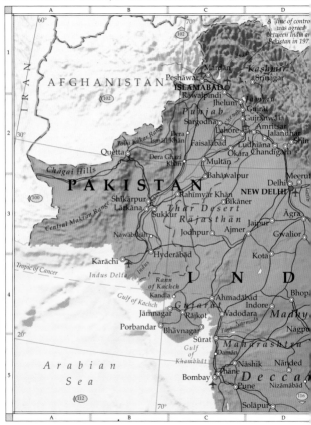

A 'line of contro
was agreed
between India an
Pakistan in 197

IRAN

AFGHANISTAN

Mardān

Peshāwar

ISLAMABAD

Rāwalpindi

Jhelum

Kashmir

Srīnagar

Jammu

Punjab

Sargodha

Gujrāt

Gujrānwāla

Amritsar

Dera Ismāīl Khan

Lahore

Jalandhar

Indu Kakar Range

Faisalābād

Ludhiāna

Shim

Quetta

Dera Ghāzi Khan

Okāra

Chandīgarh

Chagai Hills

Multān

PAKISTAN

Bahāwalpur

Delhi

Meerut

NEW DELHI

Central Makran Range

Shikārpur

Rahīmyār Khan

Bīkāner

Āgra

Lārkāna

Sukkur

Thar Desert

Jaipur

Nawābshāh

Rājasthān

Jodhpur

Ajmer

Gwalior

Karāchi

Hyderābad

Kota

Tropic of Cancer

Indus Delta

Rann
of Kachch

I N D

Kandla

Gulf of Kachch

Gujarāt

Ahmadābād

Indore

Bhop

Jāmnagar

Rājkot

Vadodara

Madhy

Porbandar

Bhāvnagar

Sūrat

Narmadā

Nāgpu

Damān

Tāpi

Mahārashtra

Gulf
of
Khambhāt

Nāshik

Nānded

Bombay

Thāne

Deccan

Pune

Nizāmābād

Arabian

Sea

Solāpur

0 km   200

0 miles   200

SOUTHERN INDIA

Arabian

Sea

Arabian Basin

70°

Thāne Nānded
Bombay
Nizāmābād
Pune
Decca
Solāpur
Hyderābā
Kṛishna
I N D I
Belgaum *Karnātaka*
Pānāji Hubli
Goa
Dāvangere
Kurnool
Bangalore Velle
Mangalore Mysore *Tam*
N a d
Amīndīvi Is.
Salem
Lakshadweep Calicut
(India) Coimbatore Tiruche
ṟāpp
Kavaratti I. Ernākulam *Kerala*
Kalpeni I. Cochin Madura
Dhanushk
Minicoy I. Trivandrum *G*
Nāgercoil *Mar*

Thiladhunmathi
Atoll

MALDIVES

MALE'

Kolhumadulu Atoll

Equator

Huvadhu Atoll

I N D

Maldive Ridge

10°

112

70°

0 km   300

0 miles   300

MAINLAND SOUTHEAST ASIA

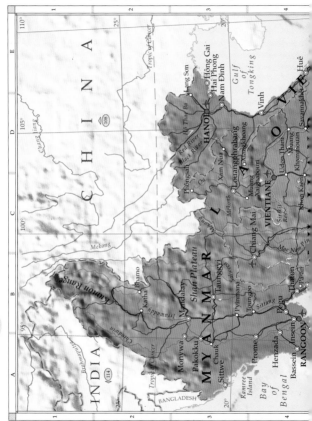

0 km   200

0 miles   200

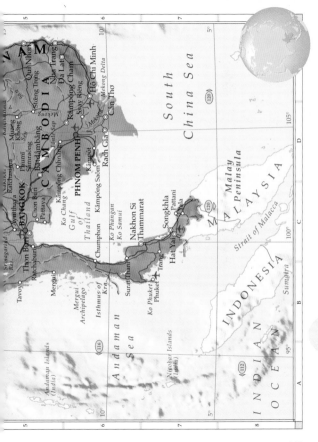

MARITIME SOUTHEAST ASIA

0 km   400

0 miles   400

E | F | G

Luzon Strait
130°

Luzon
Tuguegarao
Ilagan

Baguio

gupan
Cabanatuan
eles
MANILA **PHILIPPINES**
Lucena

angas
Mindoro
Naga Legaspi
Philippine Sea

Philippine Basin

10°

Kyushu – Palau Ridge

Mariana Trench

awan
Panay Leyte Calbayog
Samar
Iloilo Cadiz Tacloban
Cebu
Bacolod
Negros Bohol Surigao
Philippine Trench

Yap

MICRONESIA

2

rto
cesa

Iligan Cagayan de Oro
nboanga
Mindanao
Davao
General Santos

PALAU

(122)

PACIFIC OCEAN

ulu Sea
Sulu Archipelago

Celebes Sea

Kep. Talaud

Equator 0°

3

Manado

Gorontalo

Teluk Tomini

lawesi
Danau Towuti

repare
Kendari
P. Muna

jungpandang

Laut Maluku
Kep. Banggai
Kep. Sula

M a l u k u
Buru

P. Bacan

Seram

Ambon

P. Morotai

Halmahera

P. Waigeo

P. Yapen

P. Biak

Pegunungan Maoke

Pegunungan Maoke

Mamberamo

(128)

Jayapura

Irian Jaya

Digul

4

N E S I A

Banda Sea

res Sea
Flores
Kep. Alor P. Wetar
Dilo
Kep. Leti

Sumba
Timor

Kupang

Kep. Kai
Kep. Aru

Kep. Tanimbar

P. Yamdena

Timor Sea

Arafura Sea

(126)

PAPUA NEW GUINEA

5

120° | 130° | 140°

E | F | G | H

THE PACIFIC OCEAN

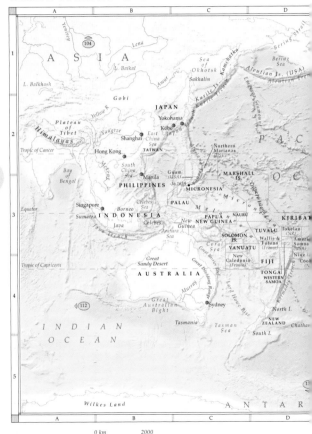

0 km   2000

0 miles   2000

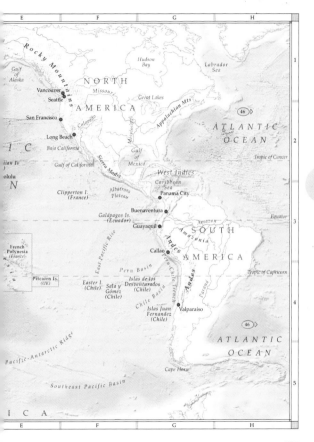

E · F · G · H

Rocky Mountains

Gulf of Alaska

Vancouver
Seattle

NORTH

AMERICA

San Francisco

Long Beach

Baja California

Sierra Madre

Gulf of California

Missouri

Great Lakes

Hudson Bay

Labrador Sea

Appalachian Mts

Colorado

Mississippi

Gulf of Mexico

West Indies

Caribbean Sea

Panama City

ATLANTIC

OCEAN

Tropic of Cancer

ian Is

olulu

N

Clipperton I.
(France)

Albatross Plateau

Galápagos Is.
(Ecuador)

Buenaventura

Guayaquil

Amazon

Amazonia

SOUTH

Equator

I C

French Polynesia
(France)

Pitcairn Is.
(UK)

East Pacific Rise

Easter I.
(Chile)

Sala y Gómez
(Chile)

Callao

Islas de los Desventurados
(Chile)

Peru Basin

Chile Basin

Andes

Andes

Peru-Chile Trench

AMERICA

Paraná

Tropic of Capricorn

Islas Juan Fernández
(Chile)

Valparaíso

Pacific-Antarctic Ridge

Southeast Pacific Basin

Cape Horn

ATLANTIC

OCEAN

I C A

46

46

123

AUSTRALASIA & OCEANIA

0 km   1000

0 miles   1000

MARSHALL IS.

Kingman Reef
(USA)

Palmyra Atoll (USA)

Baker & Howland Is.
(USA)

Jarvis Island
(USA)

Equator

PACIFIC

OCEAN

AURU

Gilbert Is.

K I R I B A T I

Phoenix Is.

Line Islands

TUVALU

Tokelau
(New Zealand)

Northern
Cook Is.

Marquesas Is.

WESTERN
SAMOA

Wallis & Futuna
(France)

NUATU

Vanua Levu

American
Samoa
(USA)

Niue
(New Zealand)

Cook Islands
(New Zealand)

French Polynesia
(France)

Viti Levu

Tahiti

Îles Loyauté

TONGA

Southern Cook Is.

Tropic of Capricorn

FIJI

Society Islands

South Fiji
Basin

Norfolk I.
(Australia)

Kermadec
Islands
(NZ)

North Cape

Bay
of
Plenty

North I.

East Cape

PACIFIC

OCEAN

Kermadec Trench

South I.

NEW
ZEALAND

Cook Strait

,550ft

Canterbury Bight

Chatham I.
(NZ)

oveaux Strait

art I.

Southwest Pacific Basin

uckland I.
NZ)

125

THE SOUTHWEST PACIFIC

MARSHALL ISLANDS

Guam (USA)
Agana

Micronesia

Mariana Trench

Yap

Caroline Islands

Chuuk Is.

Pohnpei I.

PALIKIR

Majuro

Ralik Chain
Ratak Chain

KOROR

Kosrae

PALAU

MICRONESIA

NAURU

Equator

PAPUA NEW GUINEA

Bismarck Archipelago

New Ireland

Melanesia

INDONESIA

New Guinea

Madang

Bougainville I.

Mendi

Lae

New Britain

New Georgia

PORT MORESBY

Solomon Sea

HONIARA

Santa Cruz Is.

Arafura Sea

Torres Strait

SOLOMON ISLANDS

Arnhem Land

Gulf of Carpentaria

Coral Sea

VANUATU

Bank.

NORTHERN TERRITORY

Cooktown

Cairns

Coral Sea Islands (Australia)

PORT-V

New Caledonia (France)

Tennant Creek

Normanton

Great Barrier Reef

Townsville

Mount Isa

Cloncurry

Mackay

Noumea

Iles Loya

AUSTRALIA

Longreach

Rockhampton

Alice Springs

QUEENSLAND

Great Dividing Range

Bundaberg

0 km   400

0 miles   400

WESTERN AUSTRALIA

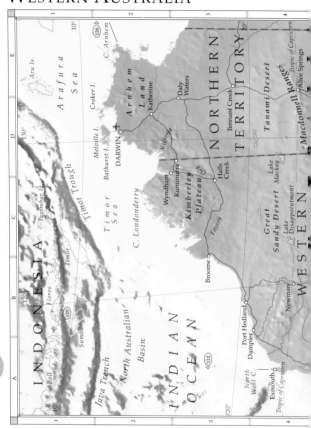

0 km   400

0 miles   400

SOUTHEAST AUSTRALIA

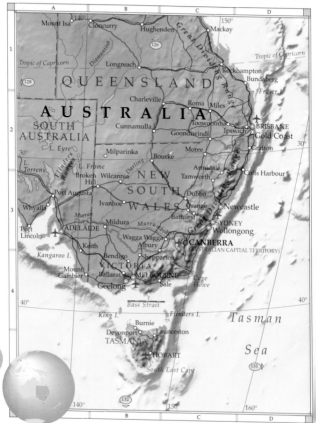

Mount Isa
Cloncurry
Hughenden
Mackay
110°
150°
126
Tropic of Capricorn
Longreach
Rockhampton
128
Bundaberg
QUEENSLAND
Fraser I.
Charleville
Roma
Miles
AUSTRALIA
Cunnamulla
Toowoomba
BRISBANE
SOUTH
Goondiwindi
Ipswich
Gold Coast
AUSTRALIA
Milparinka
Moree
Grafton
L. Eyre
Bourke
30°
L. Frome
Armidale
Coffs Harbour
L. Torrens
Broken Hill
Wilcannia
Tamworth
NEW
Port Augusta
Ivanhoe
SOUTH
Dubbo
Whyalla
WALES
Orange
Newcastle
Bathurst
Port Lincoln
Mildura
Murrumbidgee
SYDNEY
ADELAIDE
Murray
Wollongong
Wagga Wagga
CANBERRA
Keith
Albury
(AUSTRALIAN CAPITAL TERRITORY)
Kangaroo I.
Bendigo
Shepparton
Mount Gambier
Ballarat
VICTORIA
Cape Howe
Geelong
MELBOURNE
Sale
40°
Bass Strait
40°
King I.
Flinders I.
Tasman
Burnie
Devonport
Launceston
TASMANIA
Sea
131
HOBART
South East Cape
132
140°
150°
160°

0 km   400

0 miles   400

NEW ZEALAND

ANTARCTICA

ATLANTIC OCEAN

ATLANTIC

Falkland Is.
(UK)

South
Shetland Is.
(UK)

Cape
Horn

Drake Passage

Scotia Ridge

Brazillian zone of interest

South Orkney
Is. (UK)

Antarctic
Peninsula

British Antarctic Territory (UK)

Weddell
Sea

Argentina Claim

Chilean Claim

Alexander I.

Graham Land

Ronne
Ice Shelf

Vinson Massif ▲
16,864ft

Ellsworth Land

Bellingshausen Sea

Antarctic Circle

Pine
Island Bay

Marie Burd Land

Lesser
Antarctica

Amundsen Sea

Peter the First I.
(Norway)

Mt. Sidley ▲
13,718ft

Average extent of winter sea ice

PACIFIC
OCEAN

Southeast Pacific
Basin

Quee

Ritser-Larsen
Ice Shelf

A N T A

Berkner I.

South Pola
Plateau

Transantarctic Mountains

So
Po

Mount Kirkpatrick ▲
14,856ft
Mt. Markha
14,276

Ross Ice
Shelf

Cape Colbeck

Limit of permanent pack

Ross Sea

Ross Dependenc

46

44

122

0 km   750

0 miles   750

OCEAN

Limit of permanent pack ice

Maud Land *(Norway)*

Lutzow-Holm Bay

Enderby Land

Average extent of winter sea ice

RCTICA

Cape Darnley

Lambert Glacier Mackenzie Bay

Prydz Bay

Australian Antarctic Territory

Princess Elizabeth Land

Kerguelen Plateau

Antarctic Circle

Greater Antarctica

Shackleton Ice Shelf

Davis Sea

Cape Poinsett

INDIAN

OCEAN

(34)

Australian Antarctic Territory

Terre Adélie *(France)*

▲ Mt. Erebus 12,448ft

Wilkes Land

Murdo ound

▲ Mt. Siple 11,811ft

Victoria Land

(NZ)

Balleny Is.

Southwest Pacific Basin

133

GLOSSARY OF ABBREVIATIONS

This glossary provides a comprehensive guide to the abbreviations used in this Atlas.

abbrev. abbreviation
Afgh. Afghanistan
Amh. Amharic
anc. ancient
Ar. Arabic
Arm. Armenia/Armenian
Aus. Austria
Aust. Australia
Az. Azerbaijan/Azerbaijani

Bas. Basque
Bel. Belarus/Belarussian
Belg. Belgium
Bos. & Herz. Bosnia & Herzegovina
Bul. Bulgarian
Bulg. Bulgaria
Bur. Burmese

C Central
C. Cape
Cam. Cambodian
Cast. Castilian
Chin. Chinese
Cord. Cordillera (Spanish for mountain range)
Cz. Czech
Czech Rep. Czech Republic

D.C. District of Columbia
Dan. Danish
Dominican Rep. Dominican Republic

E East
Emb. Embalse
Eng. English
Est. Estonia/Estonian

Faer. Faeroese
Fin. Finnish
Flem. Flemish
Fr. France/French
ft feet

Geo. Georgia
Geor. Georgian
Ger. Germany/German
Gk. Greek

Heb. Hebrew
Hung. Hungary/Hungarian
I. Island
Ind. Indonesian
Is. Islands
It. Italian

Kaz. Kazakh
Kep. Kepulauan (Indonesian/Malay for island group)
Kir. Kirghiz
Kor. Korean
Kurd. Kurdish
Kyrgy. Kyrgyzstan

L. Lake, Lago
Lat. Latvia
Latv. Latvian
Leb. Lebanon
Liech. Liechtenstein
Lith. Lithuania/Lithuanian
Lux. Luxembourg

Mac. Macedonia
Med. Sea Mediterranean Sea
Mold. Moldova
Mt. Mount/Mountain
Mts. Mountains

N North
N. Korea North Korea
Neth. Netherlands
NW Northwest
NZ New Zealand

P. Pulau (Indonesian/Malay for island)
Peg. Pegunungan (Indonesian/Malay for mountain range)
Per. Persian
Pol. Poland/Polish
Port. Portuguese
prev. previously

R. River, Rio
Res. Reservoir
Rom. Romania/Romanian
Rus. Russian
Russ. Fed. Russian Federation

S South
S. Korea South Korea
SA South Africa
SCr. Serbo-Croatian
Slvka. Slovakia

Slvna. Slovenia
Som. Somali
Sp. Spanish
St, St. Saint
Str. Strait
Swed. Swedish
Switz. Switzerland

Tajik. Tajikistan
Th. Thai
Turk. Turkish
Turkm. Turkmen
Turkmen. Turkmenistan

U.A.E. United Arab Emirates
UK United Kingdom
Ukr. Ukrainian
USA United States of America
Uzb. Uzbek
Uzbek. Uzbekistan

var. variant
Vdkhr. Vodokhranilishche (Russian for reservoir)
Vdskh. Vodoskhovyshche (Ukrainian for reservoir)
Ven. Venezuela

W West
W. Sahara Western Sahara
Wel. Welsh

Yugo. Yugoslavia

Dorling Kindersley Cartography would like to thank the following for their assistance in producing this Atlas:

James Anderson, Laura Porter, Margaret Hynes, Ruth Duxbury, Roger Bullen, Julie Phillis, Robin Giddings and Tony Chambers.

INDEX

A

Albury Australia 130 B3

Alcácer do Sal Portugal 72 C4

Alcalá de Henares Spain 73 E3

Alchevs'k Ukraine 89 G3

Aldabra Group *Island group* Seychelles 59 G1

Aleg Mauritania 52 C3

Aleksandriya *see* Oleksandriya

Aleksandropol' *see* Gyumri

Aleksinac Yugoslavia 80 E4

Alençon France 70 B3

Alessandria Italy 76 A2

Ålesund Norway 65 A5

Aleutian Islands *Islands* Alaska, USA 16 A3

Aleutian Trench *Undersea feature* Pacific Ocean 122 D1

Alexander Island *Island* Antarctica 132 B2

Alexandretta *see* İskenderun

Alexandria Egypt 54 B1

Alexandria Louisiana, USA 28 B3

Alexandroúpoli Greece 84 D3

Al Fāshir *see* El Fasher

Alföld *Plain* Hungary 79 D7

Algarve *Region* Portugal 72 C4

Algeciras Spain 72 D5 ·

Algeria *Country* N Africa 50-51

Alghero Italy 77 A5

Algiers *Capital of* Algeria 50 D1

Al Ḥasakah Syria 98 D2

Al Ḥillah Iraq *var.* Hilla 100 B3

Al Ḥudaydah Yemen 101 B7

Al Ḥufūf Saudi Arabia 101 C5

Alicante Spain 73 F4

Alice Springs Australia 126 A5 128 E4

Al Jawf Saudi Arabia 100 B4

Al Jazīrah *Region* Iraq/Syria 98 E2

Al Jīzah *see* El Gîza

Al Karak Jordan 99 B6

Al Khārijah *see* El Khârga

Al Khums Libya 51 F2

Al Khurṭūm *see* Khartoum

Alkmaar Netherlands 66 C2

Al Kufrah Libya 51 H4

Al Lādhiqīyah Syria *Eng.* Latakia 98 B3

Allahābād India 114 C4

Allenstein *see* Olsztyn

Allentown Pennsylvania, USA 21 F4

Alma-Ata *Capital of* Kazakhstan *Rus./Kaz.* Almaty 95 C5

Al Madīnah Saudi Arabia *Eng.* Medina 100 A5

Al Mafraq Jordan 99 B5

Almalyk Uzbekistan *Uzb.* Olmaliq 103 E2

Al Manāmah *see* Manama

Al Marj Libya 51 G2

Al Mawṣil Iraq *Eng.* Mosul 100 B3

Almelo Netherlands 66 E3

Almería Spain 73 E5

Al Mukallā Yemen 101 C7

Alofi *Capital of* Niue 127 F5

Alor, Kepulauan *Island group* Indonesia 121 E5

Al Qāhirah *see* Cairo

Al Qāmishlī Syria *var.* Kamishli 98 E1

Al Qunayṭirah Syria 98 B4

Altai Mountains *Mountain Range* C Asia 106 D2

Altamura Italy 77 E5

Altay China 106 C2

Altay Mongolia 106 D2

Altun Shan *Mountain Range* China 106 B4

Alturas California, USA 24 B4

Al Wajh Saudi Arabia 100 A5

Alytus Lithuania *Pol.* Olita 87 B5

Amakusa-shotō *Island group* Japan 111 A6

Amami-Ō-shima *Island* Japan 111 A8

Amara *see* Al 'Amārah

Amarillo Texas, USA 27 E2

Amazon *River* South America 36 C2

Amazon Delta *Wetland* Brazil 36 D2

Amazonia *Region* C South America 40 C2

Ambanja Madagascar 59 G2

Ambarchik Russian Federation 95 G2

Ambato Ecuador 38 A4

Amboasary Madagascar 59 F4

Ambon Indonesia 121 F4

Ambositra Madagascar 59 G3

Ambriz Angola 58 B1

Ameland *Island* Netherlands 66 D1

American Falls Reservoir *Reservoir* Idaho, USA 24 E4

American Samoa *External territory* USA, Pacific Ocean 122 D3

Amersfoort Netherlands 66 D3

Amiens France 70 C3

Amīndīvi Islands *Island group* India 116 C3

Amirante Islands *Island group* Seychelles 59 H1

Amman *Capital of* Jordan 99 B5

Ammassalik Greenland *var.* Angmagssalik 62 C4

Ammochostos *see* Gazimağusa

Āmol Iran 100 C3

Amorgós *Island* Greece 85 D6

Amritsar India 114 D2

Amsterdam *Capital of* Netherlands 66 C3

Amstetten Austria 75 D6

Am Timan Chad 56 C3

Amu Darya *River* C Asia 102 D3

Amundsen Gulf *Sea feature* Canada 17 E2

Amundsen Sea Antarctica 132 B4

Amur *River* E Asia 93 F3 105 E1

Anadolu Dağları *see* Doğu Karadeniz Dağlari

Anadyr' Russian Federation 95 H1

Anápolis Brazil 41 F4

Anatolia *Region* SE Europe 83 G3

Anchorage Alaska, USA 16 C3

Ancona Italy 76 C3

Andalucía *Region* Spain 72 D4

Andaman Islands *Island group* India 117 H2 119 A5

Andaman Sea Indian Ocean 112 D3

Andaman-Nicobar Ridge *Undersea feature* Indian Ocean 117 H3

Andes *Mountain range* South America 37 B6

Andijon see Andizhan

Andizhan Uzbekistan *Uzb.* Andijon 103 F2

Andorra *Country* SW Europe 71 B6

Andorra la Vella *Capital of* Andorra 71 B6

Ándros *Island* Greece 85 C5

Andros Island *Island* Bahamas 34 C1

Angara *River* C Asia 93 E2

Angara Basin see Fram Basin

Ángel de la Guarda, Isla *Island* Mexico 30 B2

Angel Falls *Waterfall* Venezuela 36 C2

Angeles Philippines 121 E1

Ångermanälven *River* Sweden 64 C4

Angers France 70 B4

Anglesey *Island* Wales, UK 69 C5

Angmagssalik see Ammassalik

Angola *Country* C Africa 58

Angola Basin *Undersea feature* Atlantic Ocean 47 D5

Angora see Ankara

Angoulême France 71 B5

Angren Uzbekistan 103 E2

Anguilla *External territory* UK, West Indies 35

Anjouan *Island* Comoros 59 G2

Ankara *Capital of* Turkey *prev.* Angora 96 C3

Annaba Algeria 51 E1

An Nafūd *Desert region* Saudi Arabia 100 B4

An Najaf Iraq *var.* Najaf 100 B4

Annapolis Maryland, USA 21 F4

Ann Arbor Michigan, USA 20 C3

An Nāşirīyah Iraq *var.* Nasiriya 100 C4

Annecy France 71 D5

Anshan China 108 D4

Antakya Turkey *var.* Hatay 96 D4

Antalaha Madagascar 59 G2

Antalya Turkey *prev.* Adalia 96 B4

Antalya, Gulf of see Antalya Körfezi

Antalya Körfezi *Sea feature* Mediterranean Sea *Eng.* Gulf of Antalya, *var.* Gulf of Adalia 96 B4

Antananarivo *Capital of* Madagascar *prev.* Tananarive 59 G3

Antarctica 132-133

Antarctic Peninsula *Peninsula* Antarctica 132 A2

Antequera Spain 72 D5

Anticosti, Île d' *Island* Canada 19 E3

Antigua *Island* Antigua & Barbuda 35

Antigua & Barbuda *Country* West Indies 35

Anti-Lebanon *Mountains* Lebanon/Syria 98 B4

Antofagasta Chile 44 B2

Antsirañana Madagascar 59 G2

Antsohihy Madagascar 59 G2

Antwerp see Antwerpen

Antwerpen Belgium *Eng.* Antwerp 67 C5

Aoga-shima *Island* Japan 111 D6

Aomori Japan 110 D3

Aorangi see Cook, Mount

Aosta Italy 76 A2

Apeldoorn Netherlands 66 D3

Apennines see Appennino

Apia *Capital of* Western Samoa 127 F4

Appalachian Mountains *Mountain range* E USA 15 F4

Appennino *Mountain range* Italy *Eng.* Apennines 60 D5 76 C4

Apure *River* Venezuela 36 B2

Aputiteeq Greenland 62 D3

Aqaba *var.* Al 'Aqabah

Aqaba, Gulf of *Sea feature* Red Sea *Ar.* Khalīj al 'Aqabah 99 A8

'Aqabah, Khalīj al see Red Sea

Āqchah Afghanistan *var.* Āqchęh 102 D3

Āqchęh see Āqchah

Arabian Basin *Undersea feature* Indian Ocean 116 B2

Arabian Peninsula *Peninsula* Asia 83 H5 92 B5

Arabian Sea Indian Ocean 112 B3

Aracaju Brazil 41 H3

Arad Romania 88 A4

Arafura Sea Asia/Australasia 122 B3

Araguaia *River* Brazil 41 E3

Arāk Iran 100 C3

Araks see Aras

Arak's see Aras

Aral Sea *Inland sea* Kazakhstan/Uzbekistan 92 C3

Ararat, Mount *Peak* Turkey *var.* Great Ararat, *Turk.* Büyükağrı Dağı 92 B4

Aras *River* SW Asia *Arm.* Arak's, *Per.* Rūd-e Aras, *Rus.* Araks, *Turk.* Aras Nehri 97 G3

Aras Nehri see Aras

Arauca Colombia 38 C2

Arauca *River* Colombia/Venezuela 38 C2

Arbatax Italy 77 A5

Arbīl Iraq *Kurd.* Hawlêr 100 B3

Arctic Ocean 16-17

Arda *River* Bulgaria/Greece 84 C3

Ardennes *Region* W Europe 67 D7

Arendal Norway 65 A6

Arensburg see Kuressaare

Arequipa Peru 40 B4

Arezzo Italy 76 C3

Argentina *Country* S South America 44-45

Argentine Basin *Undersea feature* Atlantic Ocean 47 B6

Argentine claim in Antarctica 132 C2

Argentino, Lago *Lake* Argentina 45 B7

Århus Denmark 65 A7

Arica Chile 44 B1

Arizona *State* USA 26 B2

Arkansas *State* USA 28 B1

Arkansas *River* C USA 15 E4

Arkhangel'sk *Russian Federation* 90 C3 94 C2

Arles France 71 D6

Arlon Belgium 67 D8

Armenia *Country* SW Asia 97 G2

Armenia Colombia 38 B3

Armidale Australia 130 C2

Arnhem Netherlands 66 D4

Arnhem, Cape *Coastal feature* Australia 128 E2

Arnhem Land *Region* Australia 128 E2

Arno *River* Italy 76 B3

Ar Ramādī Iraq 100 B3

Arran *Island* Scotland, UK 68 C4

Ar Raqqah Syria 98 C2

Arras France 70 C2

Ar Riyāḍ *see* Riyadh

Ar Rustāq Oman *var.* Rostak 101 D5

Artesia New Mexico, USA 26 D3

Artigas Uruguay 42 B4

Aru, Kepulauan *Island group* Indonesia 121 G5

Arua Uganda 55 B6

Aruba *External territory* Netherlands, West Indies 35 E5

Arun *River* India/Nepal 115 F3

Arusha Tanzania 55 C7

Asad, Buḩayrat al *Reservoir* Syria 98 C2

Asadābād Afghanistan 103 E4

Asahikawa Japan 110 D2

Asamankese Ghana 53 E5

Ascension *Island* Atlantic Ocean 47 C5

Ascoli Piceno Italy 76 C4

Ashburton New Zealand 131 F4

Asheville North Carolina, USA 29 E1

Ashgabat *Capital of* Turkmenistan *prev.* Ashkhabad, Poltoratsk 102 B3

Ashkhabad *see* Ashgabat

Ash Shāriqah *see* Sharjah

Asia 92-93 104-105

Asmara *Capital of* Eritrea *Amh.* Asmera 54 C4

Asmera *see* Asmara

Assab Eritrea 54 D4

'Assal, Lac *see* Lac Assal

Assal, Lake *Lake* Djibouti *var.* Lac 'Assal 48 E4

As Salṭ Jordan *var.* Salt 99 B5

Assen Netherlands 66 E2

Assisi Italy 76 C4

As Sulaymānīyah Iraq 100 B3

As Sulayyil Saudi Arabia 101 B6

As Suwaydā' Syria 99 B5

Astoria Oregon, USA 24 A2

Astrakhan' Russian Federation 91 B7 95 A4

Astypálaia *Island* Greece 85 D6

Asunción *Capital of* Paraguay 42 B3

Aswān Egypt 54 B2

Asyūt Egypt 54 B2

Atacama Desert *Desert* Chile 44 B2

Atakpamé Togo 53 F4

Atâr Mauritania 52 C2

Atbara Sudan 54 C3

Athabasca, Lake *Lake* Canada 17 F4

Athens *Capital of* Greece *Gk.* Athína, *prev.* Athínai 85 C5

Athens Georgia, USA 29 E2

Athína *see* Athens

Athínai *see* Athens

Athlone Ireland 69 B5

Ati Chad 56 C3

Atlanta Georgia, USA 28 D2

Atlantic City New Jersey, USA 21 F4

Atlantic Ocean 46-47

Atlantic-Indian Basin *Undersea feature* Indian Ocean 113 A7

Atlantic-Indian Ridge *Undersea feature* Atlantic Ocean 47 D7

Atlas Mountains *Mountain range* Morocco 50 C2

Aṭ Ṭafīlah Jordan 99 B6

Aṭ Ṭā'if Saudi Arabia 100 B6

Attapu Laos 119 F5

Attawapiskat Canada 18 C3

Attawapiskat *River* Canada 18 B3

Attersee *Lake* Austria 75 D7

Attu Island *Island* Alaska, USA 16 A2

Auburn California, USA 25 B5

Auch France 71 B6

Auckland New Zealand 131 G2

Augsburg Germany 75 C6

Augusta Italy 77 D7

Augusta Georgia, USA 29 E2

Augusta Maine, USA 20 G2

Aurillac France 71 C5

Aurora Colorado, USA 22 D4

Aurora Illinois, USA 20 B3

Aussig *see* Ústí nad Labem

Austin Texas, USA 27 G4

Australasia 124-125

Australia *Country* Pacific Ocean 126-130

Australian Antarctic Territory *Territory* Antarctica 132-133

Australian Capital Territory *Territory* Australia *abbrev.* A.C.T. 130 C3

Austria *Country* C Europe 75

Auxerre France 70 C4

Avarua *Capital of* Cook Islands 127 G5

Aveiro Portugal 72 C3

Avignon France 71 D6

Ávila Spain 72 D3

Avilés Spain 72 D1

Awbārī Libya 51 F3

Axel Heiberg Island *Island* Canada 17 F1

Axios *see* Vardar

Ayacucho Peru 40 B4

Aydarkul', Ozero *Lake* Uzbekistan 102 D2

Aydın Turkey 96 A3

Ayer's Rock *see* Uluru

'Ayn ath Tha'lab Libya 51 G3

Ayr Scotland, UK 68 C4

Ayutthaya Thailand 119 C5

Ayvalık Turkey 96 A3

A'zāz Syria 98 B2

Azerbaijan *Country* SW Asia 97 G2

Azores *Islands* Portugal, Atlantic Ocean 46 C3

Azov, Sea of Black Sea *Ukr.* Azovs'ke More, *Rus.* Azovskoye More 91 A6

Azovs'ke More *see* Azov, Sea of

Azovskoye More *see* Azov, Sea of

Azul Argentina 44 D4

Azur, Côte d' *Coastal region* France 71 E6

Az Zarqā' Jordan 99 B5

Az Zāwiyah Libya 51 F2

B

Baabda Lebanon 98 B4

Baalbek Lebanon *var.* Ba'labakk 98 B4

Bab el Mandeb *Sea feature* Djibouti/Yemen 101 B7

Bābol Iran 100 D3

Babruysk Belarus *Rus.* Bobruysk 87 D6

Bacan, Pulau *Island* Indonesia 121 F4

Bačka Topola Yugoslavia 80 D2

Bacolod Philippines 121 E2

Bacău Romania 88 C4

Badain Jaran Shamo *Desert region* China 107 E3

Badajoz Spain 72 C4

Badalona Spain 73 G2

Baden Switzerland 75 E6

Bādiyat ash Shām *see* Syrian Desert

Bafatá Guinea-Bissau 52 C4

Baffin Bay *Sea feature* Atlantic Ocean 46 B1

Baffin Island *Island* Canada 15 F1

Bafoussam Cameroon 56 B4

Bagdad *see* Baghdad

Bagé Brazil 42 C4

Baghdad *Capital of* Iraq *var.* Bagdad, *Ar.* Baghdād 100 B3

Baghdād *see* Baghdad

Baghlān Afghanistan 103 E4

Baguio Philippines 121 E1

Bahamas *Country* West Indies, Atlantic Ocean 34

Baharden *see* Bakherden

Bahāwalpur Pakistan 114 C3

Bäherden *see* Bakherden

Bahía, Islas de la *Islands* Honduras 32 D2

Bahir Dar Ethiopia 54 C4

Bahrain *Country* SW Asia 101 C5

Baia Mare Romania 88 B3

Bai'an China 108 D2

Baikal, Lake *see* Baykal, Ozero

Bairiki *Capital of* Kiribati 127 E2

Baja Hungary 79 C7

Baja California *Peninsula* Mexico *Eng.* Lower California 30 B2

Bajo Nuevo *Island* Colombia 33 F2

Baker Oregon, USA 24 C3

Baker & Howland Islands *External territory* USA, Pacific Ocean 127 F2

Bakersfield California, USA 25 C7

Bakharden *see* Bakherden

Bakherden Turkmenistan *prev.* Bakharden, *var.* Baharden, *Turkm.* Bäherden 102 B3

Bākhtarān Iran *prev.* Kermānshāh 100 C3

Bakı *see* Baku

Baku *Capital of* Azerbaijan *Az.* Bakı, *var.* Baky 96 A3

Baky *see* Baku

Balabac Strait *Sea feature* South China Sea/Sulu Sea 120 D2

Ba'labakk *see* Baalbek

Balakovo Russian Federation 91 C6

Bālā Morghāb Afghanistan 102 D4

Balaton *Lake* Hungary *var.* Lake Balaton, *Ger.* Plattensee 79 C7

Balaton, Lake *see* Balaton

Balbina, Represa *Reservoir* Brazil 40 D2

Baleares, Islas *Island group* Spain *Eng.* Balearic Islands 73 H3 82 C3

Balearic Islands *see* Baleares, Islas

Bali *Island* Indonesia 120 D5

Balıkesir Turkey 96 A3

Balikpapan Indonesia 120 D4

Balkan Mountains *Mountain range* Bulgaria *Bul.* Stara Planina 84 C2

Balkhash Kazakhstan 94 C5

Balkhash, Lake *see* Balkhash, Ozero

Balkhash, Ozero *Lake* Kazakhstan *Eng.* Lake Balkhash 92 C3 94 C5

Ballarat Australia 130 B4

Balleny Islands *Island group* Antarctica 133 E5

Balsas *River* Mexico 31 E5

Bălţi Moldova 88 D3

Baltic Port *see* Paldiski

Baltic Sea Atlantic Ocean 65 C7

Baltimore Maryland, USA 21 F4

Baltischport *see* Paldiski

Baltiski *see* Paldiski

Baltiysk Kaliningrad, Russian Federation *prev.* Pillau 86 A4

Bamako *Capital of* Mali 52 D4

Bambari Central African Republic 56 C4

Bamenda Cameroon 56 B4

Banaba *Island* Kiribati *prev.* Ocean Island 127 E2

Banda, Laut *see* Banda Sea

Banda Aceh Indonesia 120 A3

Banda Sea *Sea feature* Pacific Ocean *Ind.* Laut Banda 105 E5 121 F4

Bandar-e 'Abbās Iran 100 D4

Bandar-e Büshehr Iran 100 C4

Bandar Seri Begawan *Capital of* Brunei 120 D3

Bandon Oregon, USA 24 A3

Bandundu Zaire 57 C6

Bandung Indonesia 120 C5

Bangalore India 116 D2

Banggai, Kepulauan *Island group* Indonesia 121 E4

Banghāzī Libya *Eng.* Benghazi 51 G2

Bangka, Pulau *Island* Indonesia 120 C4

Bangkok *Capital of* Thailand *Th.* Krung Thep 119 C5

Bangladesh *Country* S Asia 115

Bangor Northern Ireland, UK 69 B5

Bangor Maine, USA 21 G2

Bangui *Capital of* Central African Republic 57 C5

Bani *River* Mali 52 D3

Banī Suwayf *see* Beni Suef

Banja Luka Bosnia & Herzegovina 80 B3

Banjarmasin Indonesia 120 D4

Banjul *Capital of* Gambia 52 B3

Banks Island *Island* Canada 17 E2

Banks Island *Island* Vanuatu, Pacific Ocean 126 D4

Banská Bystrica Slovakia *Ger.* Neusohl, *Hung.* Besztercebánya 79 C6

Bantry Bay *Sea feature* Ireland 69 A6

Banyak, Kepulauan *Island group* Indonesia 120 A3

Banyo Cameroon 56 B4

Baoji China 109 B5

Baotou China 107 E3

Ba'qūbah C Iraq 100 B3

139

Baracaldo Spain 73 E1
Baranavichy Belarus *Rus.*
Baranovichi, *Pol.* Baranowicze
87 C6
Baranovichi *see* Baranavichy
Baranowicze *see* Baranavichy
Barbados Country West Indies
35 E4
Barbuda *Island* Antigua &
Barbuda 35 G3
Barcelona Spain 73 G2
Barcelona Venezuela 39 E1
Bareilly India 115 E3
Barentsburg Svalbard 63 G2
Barents Sea Arctic Ocean 64 E1
Bari Italy 77 E5
Barinas Venezuela 38 D2
Barisan, Pegunungan *Mountains*
Indonesia 120 B4
Bar-le-Duc France 70 D3
Barito *River* Indonesia 120 D4
Barlee, Lake *Lake* Australia 124
B3 129 B5
Barnaul Russian Federation
94 D4
Barnstaple England, UK 69 C7
Barquisimeto Venezuela 38 D1
Barra *Island* Scotland, UK 68 B3
Barranquilla Colombia 38 B1
Barrow *River* Ireland 69 B6
Barstow California, USA 25 C7
Bartang *River* Tajikistan 103 F3
Bartica Guyana 39 G2
Barysaw Belarus *Rus.* Borisov
87 D5
Basarabeasca Moldova 88 D4
Basel Switzerland 75 A7
Basque Provinces *Region* Spain
Sp. País Vasco 73 E1
Basra *see* Al Başrah
Bassein Myanmar 118 A4
Basse-Terre *Capital of*
Guadeloupe 35 G4
Basseterre *Capital of* St Kitts &
Nevis 35 G3
Bass Strait *Sea feature* Australia
130 B4
Bastia Corse, France 71 E7
Bastogne Belgium 67 D7
Bata Equatorial Guinea 56 A5
Batangas Philippines 121 E1
Bătdâmbâng Cambodia 119 D5

Bath England, UK 69 D7
Bathurst Australia 130 C3
Bathurst Canada 19 F4
Bathurst Island *Island* Australia
128 D2
Bathurst Island *Island* Canada
17 F2
Batman Turkey *var.* İluh 97 F2
Batna Algeria 51 E1
Baton Rouge Louisiana, USA
28 B3
Batticaloa Sri Lanka 117 E3
Bat'umi Georgia 97 F2
Bauchi Nigeria 53 G4
Bauru Brazil 42 D2
Bavarian Alps *Mountains*
Austria/Germany 75 C7
Bayamo Cuba 34 C2
Bay City Michigan, USA 20 C3
Baydhabo Somalia 55 D6
Baykal, Ozero *Lake* Russian
Federation *Eng.* Lake Baikal
93 E3 95 F4
Bayonne France 71 A6
Bayramaly Turkmenistan 102 C3
Bayrūt *see* Beirut
Beaufort Sea Arctic Ocean 17 E2
Beaufort West South Africa
58 C5
Beaumont Texas, USA 27 H4
Beauvais France 70 C3
Béchar Algeria 50 C2
Be'ér Sheva' Israel 99 A6
Beijing *Capital of* China
var. Peking 108 C4
Beira Mozambique 59 E3
Beirut *Capital of* Lebanon
var. Beyrouth, Bayrūt 98 B4
Beja Portugal 72 C4
Béjaïa Algeria 51 E1
Bek-Budi *see* Karshi
Békéscsaba Hungary 79 D7
Belarus Country E Europe *var.*
Belorussia 87
Belau see Palau
Belcher Islands *Islands* Canada
18 C2
Beledweyne Somalia 55 D5
Belém Brazil 41 F2
Belfast Northern Ireland, UK
69 B5
Belfort France 70 E4

Belgaum India 116 C1
Belgium Country W Europe 67
Belgorod Russian Federation
91 A5
Belgrade *Capital of* Yugoslavia
SCr. Beograd 80 D3
Belitung, Pulau *Island* Indonesia
120 C4
Belize Country Central
America 32
Belize City Belize 32 C1
Bella Unión Uruguay 42 B4
Belle Île *Island* France 70 A4
Belle Isle, Strait of *Sea feature*
Canada 15 G3 19 H3
Bellevue Washington, USA
24 B2
Bellingham Washington, USA
24 B1
Bellingshausen Sea Antarctica
47 A8 132 A3
Bello Colombia 38 B2
Belluno Italy 76 C2
Bellville South Africa 58 C5
Belmopan *Capital of* Belize 32 C1
Belo Horizonte Brazil 41 G5
43 F1
Belorussia *see* Belarus
Belostok *see* Białystok
Beloye More Arctic Ocean
Eng. White Sea 61 F1 90 C3
Bend Oregon, USA 24 B3
Bendery *see* Tighina
Bendigo Australia 130 B4
Benevento Italy 77 D5
Bengal, Bay of *Sea feature* Indian
Ocean 112 C3
Benghazi *see* Banghāzī
Bengkulu Indonesia 120 B4
Benguela Angola 58 B2
Beni *River* Bolivia 40 C4
Benidorm Spain 73 F4
Beni Mellal Morocco 50 C2
Benin Country N Africa *prev.*
Dahomey 53
Benin, Bight of *Sea feature* W
Africa 53 F5
Benin City Nigeria 53 F5
Beni Suef Egypt *var.* Banī
Suwayf 54 B1
Benue *River* Cameroon/Nigeria
53 G4
Beograd *see* Belgrade

Berat Albania 81 B3

Berbera Somalia 54 D4

Berbérati Central African Republic 56 C5

Berdyans'k Ukraine 88 G4

Berezina *see* Byerazino

Bergamo Italy 76 B2

Bergen Norway 65 A5

Bering Sea Pacific Ocean 122 D1

Bering Strait *Sea feature* Bering Sea/Chukchi Sea 122 D1

Berkner Island *Island* Antarctica 132 C2

Berlin *Capital of* Germany 74 D3

Bermejo *River* Argentina 44 D2

Bermuda *External territory* UK, Atlantic Ocean 46 B3

Bern *Capital of* Switzerland *Fr.* Berne 75 A7

Berne *see* Bern

Bertoua Cameroon 57 B5

Besançon France 70 D4

Besztercebánya *see* Banská Bystrica

Bethlehem West Bank 99 B5

Beuthen *see* Bytom

Beyrouth *see* Beirut

Béziers France 71 C6

Bezmein *see* Byuzmeyin

Bhamo Myanmar 118 B2

Bhātāpāra India 114 C4

Bhāvnagar India 114 C4

Bhōpāl India 114 D4

Bhutan *Country* S Asia 115

Biak, Pulau *Island* Indonesia 121 G4

Białystok Poland *Rus.* Belostok 78 E3

Biel Switzerland 75 A7

Bielitz-Biala *see* Bielsko-Biała

Bielsko-Biała Poland *Ger.* Bielitz-Biala 79 C5

Bighorn Mountains *Mountains* C USA 22 C2

Big Spring Texas, USA 27 E3

Bihać Bosnia & Herzegovina 80 B3

Bihār *State* India 115 F3

Bijelo Polje Yugoslavia 80 D4

Bīkaner India 114 C3

Bila Tserkva Ukraine 89 E2

Bilbao Spain 73 E1

Billings Montana, USA 22 C2

Biloxi Mississippi, USA 28 C3

Biltine Chad 56 D3

Binghamton New York, USA 21 F3

Bío Bío *River* Chile 45 B5

Birāk Libya 51 F3

Biratnagar Nepal 115 F3

Bīrganj Nepal 115 F3

Birmingham England, UK 69 D6

Birmingham Alabama, USA 28 D2

Birni-Nkonni Niger 53 F3

Birsen *see* Biržai

Biržai Lithuania *Ger.* Birsen 86 C4

Biscay, Bay of *Sea feature* Atlantic Ocean 71 A5 73 E1

Biscay Plain *Undersea feature* Atlantic Ocean 60 B4

Bishkek *Capital of* Kyrgyzstan *prev.* Frunze, Pishpek 103 F2

Bishop California, USA 25 C6

Biskra Algeria 51 E2

Bismarck North Dakota, USA 23 E2

Bismarck Archipelago *Island group* Papua New Guinea 126 B3

Bissau *Capital of* Guinea-Bissau 52 B4

Bitola Macedonia 81 D6

Bitterroot Range *Mountains* NW USA 24 D2

Biwa-ko *Lake* Japan 111 C5

Bjelovar Croatia 80 B2

Black Drin *River* Albania/Macedonia 81 D5

Black Forest *see* Schwarzwald

Black Hills *Mountains* C USA 22 D3

Blackpool England, UK 69 C5

Black River *River* China/Vietnam 118 D3

Black Sea Asia/Europe 61 F1 82 B4

Black Volta *River* Ghana/Ivory Coast 53 E4

Blackwater *River* Ireland 69 A6

Blagoevgrad Bulgaria 84 B3

Blagoveshchensk Russian Federation 95 G4

Blanca, Bahía *Sea feature* Argentina 37 C6

Blantyre Malawi 59 E2

Blenheim New Zealand 131 G3

Blida Algeria 50 D1

Bloemfontein South Africa 58 D4

Blois France 70 C4

Bloomington Indiana, USA 20 C4

Bluefields Nicaragua 33 E3

Blue Mountains *Mountains* W USA 24 C3

Blue Nile *River* Ethiopia/Sudan 55 C4

Blumenau Brazil 42 D3

Bo Sierra Leone 52 C4

Boa Vista Brazil 40 D1

Bobo-Dioulasso Burkina 53 E4

Bobruysk *see* Babruysk

Boca de la Serpiente *see* Serpent's Mouth, The

Bochum Germany 74 A4

Bodø Norway 64 C3

Bodrum Turkey 94 A4

Bogor Indonesia 120 C5

Bogotá *Capital of* Colombia 38 B3

Bo Hai *Sea feature* Yellow Sea 108 D4

Bohemian Forest *Region* Czech Rep 75 D6

Bohol *Island* Philippines 121 E2

Boise Idaho, USA 24 D3

Bokhara *see* Bukhara

Bol Chad 56 B3

Bolivia *Country* C South America 40-41

Bologna Italy 76 C3

Bolton England, UK 69 D5

Bolzano Italy *Ger.* Bozen 76 C1

Boma Zaire 57 B7

Bombay India *var.* Mumbai 115 C5 116 C1

Bomu *River* Central African Republic/Zaire 57 D5

Bonete, Cerro *Peak* Chile 37 B5

Bongo, Massif de *Upland* Central African Republic 56 D4

Bongor Chad 56 C3

Bonn Germany 75 A5

Boosaaso Somalia 54 E4

141

Bujumbura *Capital of* Burundi
prev. Usumbura 55 B7

Bukavu Zaire 57 E6

Bukhara Uzbekistan *var.*
Bokhara, *Uzb.* Bukhoro 102 D2

Bukhoro *see* Bukhara

Bulawayo Zimbabwe 58 D3

Bulgaria *Country* E Europe 84

Bumba Zaire 57 D5

Bunbury Australia 129 B6

Bundaberg Australia 126 C5
130 C1

Bunia Zaire 57 E5

Buraydah Saudi Arabia 101 B5

Burë Ethiopia 54 C4

Burgas Bulgaria 84 E2

Burgos Spain 73 E2

Burgundy *see* Bourgogne

Burkina *Country* W Africa 53

Burlington Iowa, USA 23 G4

Burlington Vermont, USA 21 F2

Burma *see* Myanmar

Burnie Tasmania 130 B4

Burns Oregon, USA 24 C3

Bursa Turkey *prev.* Brusa 96 B3

Burtnieku Ezers *Lake* Latvia
86 C3

Buru *Island* Indonesia 121 F4

Burundi *Country* C Africa 55

Butembo Zaire 57 E5

Butte Montana, USA 22 B2

Butuan Philippines 121 F2

Buurhakaba Somalia 55 D6

Buyo Reservoir *Reservoir* Ivory
Coast 52 D5

Büyükağrı Dağı *see* Ararat,
Mount

Buzău Romania 88 C4

Bydgoszcz Poland *Ger.*
Bromberg 78 C3

Byerazino *River* Belarus *Rus.*
Berezina 87 B6

Bykhaw Belarus *Rus.* Bykhov
87 D6

Bykhov *see* Bykhaw

Bytom Poland *Ger.* Beuthen
79 C5

Byuzmeyin Turkmenistan *prev.*
Bezmein 102 B3

Byzantium *see* İstanbul

C

Caaguazú Paraguay 42 C2

Cabanatuan Philippines 121 E1

Cabimas Venezuela 38 C1

Cabinda *Exclave* Angola 57 B7
58 B1

Cabot Strait *Sea feature* Atlantic
Ocean 19 G4

Čačak Yugoslavia 80 D4

Cáceres Spain 72 D3

Cachoeiro de Itapemirim Brazil
43 F1

Cadiz Philippines 121 E2

Cádiz Spain 72 D5

Caen France 70 B3

Caernarfon Wales, UK 69 C5

Cagayan de Oro Philippines
121 F2

Cagliari Italy 77 A6

Cahors France 71 B5

Cairns Australia 126 B4

Cairo *Capital of* Egypt *Ar.* Al
Qāhirah, *var.* El Qâhira 54 B1

Čakovec Croatia 80 B2

Calabar Nigeria 53 G5

Calabria *Region* Italy 77 D6

Calafate Argentina 45 B7

Calais France 70 C2

Calais Maine, USA 21 H1

Calama Chile 44 B2

Calbayog Philippines 121 F2

Calcutta India 115 F4

Caldas da Rainha Portugal
72 B3

Caldwell Idaho, USA 25 C3

Caleta Olivia Argentina 45 C6

Calgary Canada 17 E5

Cali Colombia 38 B3

Calicut India *var.* Kozhikode
116 D2

California *State* USA 24-25

California, Golfo de *Sea feature*
Pacific Ocean *Eng.* California,
Gulf of 30 B2 123 F2

Callao Peru 40 A4

Caltagirone Italy 77 D7

Caltanissetta Italy 77 C7

Camagüey Cuba 34 C2

Cambodia *Country* SE Asia
Cam. Kampuchea 118-119

Cambridge England, UK 69 E6

Cameroon *Country* W Africa
56-57

Camiri Bolivia 40 D5

Campbell Plateau *Undersea feature* Pacific Ocean 131 H4

Campeche Mexico 31 H4

Campeche, Bahía de *Sea feature*
Mexico *Eng.* Gulf of
Campeche 31G4

Campina Grande Brazil 41 H3

Campinas Brazil 41 F5 43 E2

Campo Grande Brazil 41 E5
42 C1

Campos Brazil 41 G5 43 F2

Canada *Country* North America
16-17 18-19

Canada Basin *Undersea feature*
Arctic Ocean *var.* Laurentian
Basin 12 B4

Canadian River *River* SW USA
27 E2

Çanakkale Turkey 96 A2

Çanakkale Boğazı *see*
Dardanelles

Canarias, Islas *Islands* Spain
Eng. Canary Islands 46
C4 50 A2

Canary Basin *Undersea feature*
Atlantic Ocean 46 C4

Canary Islands *see* Canarias,
Islas

Canaveral, Cape *Coastal feature*
Florida, USA 29 F4

Canberra *Capital of* Australia
130 C3

Cancún Mexico 31 H3

Caniapiscau *River* Canada 19 E2

Caniapiscau, Réservoir *Reservoir*
Canada 19 E3

Canik Dağları *Mountains* Turkey
96 D2

Çankırı Turkey 96 C2

Cannes France 71 D6

Canoas Brazil 42 D4

Canterbury England, UK 69 E7

Canterbury Bight *Sea feature*
Pacific Ocean 131 G4

Canterbury Plains *Plain* New
Zealand 131 G4

Cân Tho Vietnam 119 D6

Canton Ohio, USA 20 D4

Canton *see* Guangzhou

Cape Basin *Undersea feature*
Atlantic Ocean 49 C7 58 B5

Courantyne *River*
Guyana/Suriname
var. Corantijn 39 G3

Courland Lagoon *Sea feature*
Baltic Sea 86 A4

Coventry England, UK 69 D6

Covilhã Portugal 72 C3

Cozumel, Isla de *Island* Mexico
31 H3

Cracow *see* Kraków

Craiova Romania 88 B5

Cremona Italy 76 B2

Cres *Island* Croatia 80 A3

Crescent City California, USA
24 A4

Crete Greece *see* Kríti 83 F4

Crete, Sea of Mediterranean Sea
Gk. Kritikó Pélagos 85 D5

Crimea *Peninsula* Ukraine
var. Krym 88 F4

Croatia *Country* SE Europe 80

Croker Island *Island* Australia
128 D2

Crotone Italy 77 E6

Crozet Basin *Undersea feature*
Indian Ocean 113 B6

Crozet Islands *Island group*
Indian Ocean 113 B6

Cruzeiro do Sul Brazil 40 B3

Cuanza *River* Angola 58 B1

Cuba *Country* West Indies 34

Cubango *see* Okavango

Cúcuta Colombia 38 C2

Cuenca Ecuador 38 A5

Cuenca Spain 73 E3

Cuernavaca Mexico 31 E4

Cuiabá Brazil 41 E4

Cuito *River* Angola 58 C2

Culiacán Mexico 30 C3

Cumaná Venezuela 39 E1

Cumberland Maryland, USA
21 E4

Cumberland *River* C USA 20 C5

Cunene *River* Angola/Namibia
58 B2

Cunnamulla Australia 130 B2

Curicó Chile 44 B4

Curitiba Brazil 42 D3

Cusco Peru *prev.* Cuzco 40 B4

Cuttack India 115 F5

Cuxhaven Germany 74 B3

Cuyuni *River*
Guyana/Venezuela 39 F2

Cuzco *see* Cusco

Cyclades *see* Kykládes

Cymru *see* Wales

Cyprus *Country* Mediterranean
Sea 96 C5

Czechoslovakia *see* Czech
Republic *or* Slovakia

Czech Republic *Country*
C Europe 78-79

Częstochowa Poland
Ger. Tschenstochau 78 C4

D

Dacca *see* Dhaka

Dagden *see* Hiiumaa

Dagö *see* Hiiumaa

Dagupan Philippines 121 E1

Da Hinggan Ling *Mountain
range* China *Eng.* Great
Khingan Range 107 G1

Dahomey *see* Benin

Dakar *Capital* of Senegal 52 B3

Đakovo Croatia 80 C3

Dalaman Turkey 96 B4

Đa Lat Vietnam 119 E5

Dali China 109 A6

Dalian China 108 D4

Dallas Texas, USA 27 G3

Dalmacija *Region* Croatia
80 B4

Daloa Ivory Coast 52 D5

Daly Waters Australia 128 E3

Damān India 114 C5

Damas *see* Damascus

Damascus Syria *var.* Esh Sham,
Fr. Damas, *Ar.* Dimashq 98 B4

Dampier Australia 128 B4

Đa Năng Vietnam 119 E4

Daneborg Greenland 63 E3

Dangara Tajikistan 103 E3

Danmarkshavn Greenland 63 E2

Danmarksstraedet *see* Denmark
Strait

Danube *River* C Europe 60 D4

Danube Delta *Wetland*
Romania/Ukraine 88 D5

Danville Virginia, USA 21 E5

Danzig *see* Gdańsk

Darʿā Syria 99 B5

Dardanelles *Sea feature* Turkey
Turk. Çanakkale Boğazı 96 A2

Dar es Salaam Tanzania 55 C8

Darhan Mongolia 107 E2

Darien, Gulf of *Sea feature*
Caribbean Sea 33 G5

Darling *River* Australia 130 B2

Darmstadt Germany 75 B5

Darnah Libya 51 H2

Darnley, Cape *Coastal feature*
Antarctica 133 G2

Dartmoor *Region* England, UK
69 C7

Dartmouth Canada 19 G4

Darwin Australia 128 D2

Dashhowuz *see* Dashkhovuz

Dashhowuz Turkmenistan
prev. Tashauz, *Turkm.*
Dashhowuz 102 C2

Datong China 108 C4

Daugava *see* Western Dvina

Daugavpils Latvia *Ger.*
Dünaburg, *Rus.* Dvinsk 86 C4

Dāvangere India 116 D2

Davao Philippines 121 F2

Davenport Iowa, USA 23 G3

David Panama 33 E5

Davis Sea Indian Ocean 133 H3

Davis Strait *Sea feature* Atlantic
Ocean 17 H2 62 B4

Dawson Canada 16 D3

Dayr az Zawr Syria 98 D3

Dayton Ohio, USA 20 C4

Daytona Beach Florida, USA
29 F4

Dead Sea *Salt Lake* SW Asia
Ar. Al Baḥr al Mayyit, Baḥrat
Lūṭ, *Heb.* Yam HaMelah 99 B5

Death Valley *Valley* W USA
14 D4 25 D6

Debre Zeyit Ethiopia 55 C5

Debrecen Hungary *prev.*
Debreczen, *Ger.* Debreczin
79 D6

Debreczen *see* Debrecen

Debreczin *see* Debrecen

Decatur Illinois, USA 20 B4

Deccan *Plateau* India 104 B3

Děčín Czech Republic
Ger. Tetschen 78 B4

Dej Romania 88 B3

Delaware *State* USA 21 F4

Delaware Bay *Sea feature* USA
21 F4

Delémont Switzerland 75 A7

147

Delft Netherlands 66 B4
Delfzijl Netherlands 66 E1
Delhi India 114 D3
Del Rio Texas, USA 27 F4
Demchok *Disputed region*
China/India *var.* Dêmqog 106
A4 115 E2
Dêmqog *see* Demchok
Denali *Peak* Alaska, USA
prev. Mount McKinley 14 C2
Den Helder Netherlands 66 C2
Denizli Turkey 96 B4
Denmark *Country* NW
Europe 65
Denmark Strait *Sea feature*
Greenland/Iceland *var.*
Danmarksstraedet 63 D3
Denpasar Indonesia 120 D5
Denton Texas, USA 27 G2
Denver Colorado, USA 22 D4
Dera Ghāzi Khān Pakistan
114 C2
Dera Ismāīl Khān Pakistan
114 C2
Derby England, UK 69 D6
Derg, Lough *Lake* Ireland 69 B6
Desē Ethiopia 54 D4
Deseado *River* Argentina
45 C6
Des Moines Iowa, USA 23 F3
Despoto Planina *see* Rhodope
Mountains
Dessau Germany 74 C4
Desventurados, Islas de los
Islands Chile 37 A5 123 G4
Detroit Michigan, USA 20 D3
Deutschendorf *see* Poprad
Deva Romania 88 B4
Deventer Netherlands 66 D3
Devollit, Lumi i *River* Albania
81 D6
Devon Island *Island* Canada
17 G2
Devonport Tasmania, Australia
130 B5
Dezfūl Iran 100 C3
Dhaka *Capital of* Bangladesh
var. Dacca 115 G4
Dhanbād India 115 F4
Dhanushkodi India 116 D3
Dhrepanon, Ákra *Coastal feature*
Greece 84 C4
Diamantina *River* Australia
130 B1

Dickinson North Dakota, USA
22 D2
Diekirch Luxembourg 67 D7
Dieppe France 70 C3
Diffa Niger 53 H3
Digul *River* Indonesia 121 H5
Dijon France 70 D4
Dīla Ethiopia 55 C5
Dili Indonesia 121 F5
Dilling Sudan 54 B4
Dilolo Zaire 57 D8
Dimashq *see* Damascus
Dimitrovo *see* Pernik
Dinant Belgium 67 C7
Dinara *Mountains* Bosnia &
Herzegovina/Croatia 80 B4
Dingle Bay *Sea feature* Ireland
69 A5
Diourbel Senegal 52 B3
Dirē Dawa Ethiopia 55 D5
Dirk Hartog Island *Island*
Australia 129 A5
Disappointment, Lake *Salt lake*
Australia 118 C4
Dispur India 115 G3
Divinópolis Brazil 43 F1
Diyarbakır Turkey 97 E4
Djambala Congo 57 B6
Djibouti *Country* E Africa 54
Djibouti *Capital of* Djibouti
var. Jibuti 54 D4
Djúpivogur Iceland 63 E4
Dnieper *River* E Europe 51 F4
Dniester *River*
Moldova/Ukraine 88 D3
Dnipropetrovs'k Ukraine
89 F3
Dobele Latvia *Ger.* Doblen
86 B3
Doblen *see* Dobele
Doboj Bosnia & Herzegovina
80 C3
Dobrich Bulgaria 84 E1
Dodecanese *see* Dodekánisos
Dodekánisos *Islands* Greece
Eng. Dodecanese 85 E6
Dodge City Kansas, USA 23 E5
Dodoma *Capital of* Tanzania
55 C7
Doğu Karadeniz Dağları
Mountains Turkey
var. Anadolu Dağları 97 E2
Doha *Capital of* Qatar
Ar. Ad Dawḩah 101 C5

Dolomites *see* Dolomiti
Dolomiti *Mountains* Italy
Eng. Dolomites 76 C2
Dolores Argentina 44 D4
Dominica *Country* West
Indies 35
Dominican Republic *Country*
West Indies 35
Don *River* Russian Federation
94 A3
Donegal Bay *Sea feature* Ireland
69 A5
Donets *River* Russian
Federation/Ukraine 88 G3
91 A6
Donets'k Ukraine 89 G3
Dongola Sudan 54 B3
Dongting Hu *Lake* China
109 C6
Donostia *see* San Sebastián
Dordogne *River* France
71 B5
Dordrecht Netherlands 66 C4
Dornbirn Austria 75 B7
Dorpat *see* Tartu
Dortmund Germany 74 A4
Dosso Niger 53 F3
Dothan Alabama, USA 28 D3
Douai France 70 C2
Douala Cameroon 57 A5
Douglas UK 69 C5
Douglas Arizona, USA 26 C3
Dourados Brazil 42 C2
Douro *River* Portugal/Spain
Sp. Duero 72 C2
Dover England, UK 69 E7
Dover Delaware, USA 21 F4
Dōzen *Island* Japan 111 B5
Drakensberg *Mountain range*
Lesotho/South Africa
58 D5
Drake Passage *Sea feature*
Atlantic Ocean/Pacific Ocean
37 C8
Dráma Greece 84 C3
Drammen Norway 65 B6
Drau *River* C Europe *var.* Drava
75 D7 80 C3
Drava *River* C Europe *var.* Drau
79 C7
Dresden Germany 74 D4
Drina *River* Bosnia &
Herzegovina/Yugoslavia
80 D4

Drobeta-Turnu Severin Romania *prev.* Turnu Severin 88 B4

Druskieniki *see* Druskininkai

Druskininkai Lithuania *Pol.* Druskieniki 87 B5

Dubai United Arab Emirates 101 D5

Dubăsari Moldova 88 D3

Dubawnt *River* Canada 17 F4

Dubbo Australia 130 C3

Dublin *Capital of* Ireland 69 B5

Dubrovnik Croatia 81 C5

Dubuque Iowa, USA 23 G3

Duero *River* Portugal/Spain *Port.* Douro 72 D2

Dugi Otok *Island* Croatia 80 A4

Duisburg Germany 74 A4

Duluth Minnesota, USA 23 F2

Dumfries Scotland, UK 68 C4

Düna *see* Western Dvina

Dünaburg *see* Daugavpils

Dundalk Ireland 69 B5

Dundee Scotland, UK 68 C3

Dunedin New Zealand 131 F5

Dunkerque France *Eng.* Dunkirk 70 C2

Dunkirk *see* Dunkerque

Duqm Oman 101 E6

Durango Mexico 30 D3

Durango Colorado, USA 22 C5

Durazno Uruguay 42 C5

Durban South Africa 58 E4

Durham North Carolina, USA 29 F1

Durrës Albania 81 C6

Dushanbe *Capital of* Tajikistan *var.* Dyushambe, *prev.* Stalinabad 103 E3

Düsseldorf Germany 74 A4

Dutch Harbor Alaska, USA 16 B3

Dutch West Indies *see* Netherland Antilles

Dvina *River* E Europe 61 E3

Dvinsk *see* Daugavpils

Dyushambe *see* Dushanbe

Dzaudzhikau *see* Vladikavkaz

Dzhalal-Abad Kyrgyzstan *Kir.* Jalal-Abad 103 F2

Dzhambul *see* Zhambyl

Dzhezkazgan *see* Zhezkazgan

Dzhugdzhur Range *Mountain range* Russian Federation 93 F3

Dzvina *see* Western Dvina

E

Eagle Pass Texas, USA 27 F4

East Cape *Coastal feature* New Zealand 131 H2

East China Sea Pacific Ocean 122 B2

Easter Island *Island* Pacific Ocean 123 F4

Eastern Ghats *Mountain range* India 104 B4

Eastern Sierra Madre *see* Sierra Madre Oriental

East Falkland *Island* Falkland Islands 45 D7

East Frisian Islands *see* Ostfriesische Inseln

East London South Africa 58 D5

Eastmain *River* Canada 18 D3

East Pacific Rise *Undersea feature* Pacific Ocean 123 F3

East Siberian Sea *see* Vostochno-Sibirskoye More

East St Louis Illinois, USA 20 B4

Eau Claire Wisconsin, USA 20 A2

Ebolowa Cameroon 57 B5

Ebro *River* Spain 73 F2

Ecuador *Country* NW South America 38

Ed Eritrea 54 D4

Ede Netherlands 66 D3

Ede Nigeria 53 F4

Edgeøya *Island* Svalbard 63 H2

Edinburgh Scotland, UK 68 C4

Edirne Turkey 96 A2

Edmonton Canada 17 E5

Edward, Lake *Lake* Uganda/Zaire 57 E6

Edwards Plateau *Upland* S USA 27 F4

Eforie-Nord Romania 88 D5

Egadi, Isole *Island group* Italy 77 B7

Ege Denizi *see* Aegean Sea

Eger *see* Ohře

Egiyn Gol *River* Mongolia 106 D2

Egypt *Country* NE Africa 54

Eindhoven Netherlands 67 D5

Eisenstadt Austria 75 E7

Eivissa *Island* Spain *Cast.* Ibiza 73 G4

Elat Israel 99 B7

Elâzığ Turkey 97 E3

Elba, Isola d' *Island* Italy 76 B4

Elbasan Albania 81 D6

Elbe *River* Czech Republic/Germany 79 B5

Elbing *see* Elbląg

Elbląg Poland *Ger.* Elbing 78 C2

El'brus *Peak* Russian Federation 61 G4 83 H2

Elche Spain 73 F4

Elda Spain 73 F4

Eldoret Kenya 55 C6

Eleuthera *Island* Bahamas 34 C1

El Fasher Sudan *var.* Al Fāshir 54 A4

Elgin Scotland, UK 68 C3

El Gîza Egypt *var.* Al Jīzah 54 B1

Elista Russian Federation 91 B7

El Khârga Egypt *var.* Al Khārijah 54 B2

Elko Nevada, USA 25 D5

Ellensburg Washington, USA 24 B2

Ellesmere Island *Island* Canada 17 F1

Ellsworth Land *Region* Antarctica 132 B3

El Minya Egypt 54 B2

Elmira New York, USA 21 E3

El Obeid Sudan 54 B4

El Paso Texas, USA 26 D3

El Qâhira *see* Cairo

El Salvador *Country* Central America 32

El Tigre Venezuela 39 E2

Ely NV USA 25 D5

Emden Germany 74 A3

Emmen Netherlands 66 E2

Emperor Seamount *Undersea feature* Pacific Ocean 122 D2

Empty Quarter *see* Rub' al Khali

Ems *River* Germany/Netherlands 74 A3

Encarnación Paraguay 42 C3

Finisterre, Cape *Coastal feature* Spain 72 B1

Finland *Country* N Europe 64-65

Finland, Gulf of *Sea feature* Baltic Sea 65 E6

Firenze Italy *Eng.* Florence 76 B3

Fish *River* Namibia 58 C4

Fishguard Wales, UK 69 C6

Fitzroy *River* Australia 124 B2 128 C3

Fiume *see* Rijeka

Flagstaff Arizona, USA 26 B2

Flanders *Region* Belgium 67 A5

Flensburg Germany 74 B2

Flinders Island *Island* Australia 130 B4

Flinders Ranges *Mountain range* Australia 130 A2

Flin Flon Canada 17 F5

Flint Michigan, USA 20 C4

Flint Island *Island* Kiribati 127 H4

Florence Alabama, USA 28 C2

Florence South Carolina, USA 29 F2

Florence *see* Firenze

Florencia Colombia 38 B3

Flores Guatemala 32 B1

Flores Indonesia 121 E5

Flores, Laut *see* Flores Sea

Flores Sea *Pacific Ocean Ind.* Laut Flores 121 E5

Florianópolis Brazil 42 D3

Florida *State* USA 29 E4

Florida, Straits of *Sea feature* Bahamas/USA 29 F5 34 B1

Floridablanca Colombia 38 C2

Florida Keys *Island chain* Florida, USA 29 F5

Flórina Greece 84 A3

Flushing *see* Vlissingen

Foča Bosnia & Herzegovina 80 C4

Focşani Romania 88 C4

Foggia Italy 77 D5

Fongafale *Capital of* Tuvalu 127 H3

Fonseca, Gulf of *Sea feature* El Salvador/Honduras 32 C3

Forlì Italy 76 C3

Formentera *Island* Spain 73 G4

Former Yugoslav Republic of Macedonia *see* Macedonia

Formosa Argentina 44 D2

Formosa *see* Taiwan

Formosa Strait *see* Taiwan Strait

Føroyar *see* Faeroe Islands

Fortaleza Brazil 41 H2

Fort Collins Colorado, USA 22 D4

Fort-de-France *Capital of* Martinique 35 G4

Forth *River* Scotland, UK 68 C4

Forth, Firth of *Inlet* Scotland, UK 68 D4

Fort Lauderdale Florida, USA 29 F5

Fort McMurray Canada 17 F4

Fort Myers Florida, USA 29 E5

Fort Peck Lake *Lake* Montana, USA 22 C1

Fort Saint John Canada 17 E4

Fort Smith Canada 17 F4

Fort Smith Arkansas, USA 28 A1

Fort Wayne Indiana, USA 20 C4

Fort William Scotland, UK 68 C3

Fort Worth Texas, USA 27 G3

Foveaux Strait *Sea feature* New Zealand 131 E5

Fram Basin *Undersea feature* Arctic Ocean *var.* Angara Basin 12 C4

Franca Brazil 43 E1

Francistown Botswana 58 D3

Frankfort Kentucky, USA 20 C5

Frankfurt *see* Frankfurt am Main

Frankfurt am Main Germany *Eng.* Frankfurt 75 B5

Frankfurt an der Oder Germany 74 D4

Fränkische Alb *Mountains* Germany 75 C6

Frantsa-Iosifa, Zemlya *Islands* Russian Federation *Eng.* Franz Josef Land 13 D6 94 D1

Franz Josef Land *see* Frantsa-Iosifa, Zemlya

Fraser Island *Island* Australia 130 D1

Frauenburg *see* Saldus

Fray Bentos Uruguay 42 B5

Fredericton Canada 19 F4

Frederikshavn Denmark 65 B7

Fredrikstad Norway 65 B6

Freeport Bahamas 34 C1

Freeport Texas, USA 27 G4

Freetown *Capital of* Sierra Leone 52 C4

Freiburg im Breisgau Germany 75 B7

Fremantle Australia 129 B6

French Guiana *External territory* France, N South America 39

French Polynesia *External territory* France, Pacific Ocean 123 E3

Fresno California, USA 25 B6

Fribourg Switzerland 75 A7

Frome, Lake *Lake* Australia 130 A2

Frosinone Italy 76 C4

Frunze *see* Bishkek

Fuerteventura *Island* Spain 50 A3

Fuji, Mount *Peak* Japan 105 E2

Fukui Japan 111 C5

Fukuoka Japan 111 A6

Fukushima Japan 110 D3

Fulda Germany 75 B5

Fünfkirchen *see* Pécs

Furnas, Represa de *Reservoir* Brazil 43 E1

Fuzhou China 109 D6

FYR Macedonia *see* Macedonia

G

Gaalkacyo Somalia 55 E5

Gabès Tunisia 51 E2

Gabon *Country* W Africa 57

Gaborone *Capital of* Botswana 58 D4

Gabrovo Bulgaria 84 D2

Gadsden Alabama, USA 28 C2

Gaeta, Golfo di *Sea feature* Italy 77 C5

Gafsa Tunisia 51 E2

Gagnoa Ivory Coast 52 D5

Gagra Georgia 97 E1

Gairdner, Lake *Lake* Australia 129 E6

Galapagos Islands *Islands*
Ecuador, Pacific Ocean
var. Tortoise Islands, *Sp.*
Archipiélago de Colón 36 A2

Galaţi Romania 88 D4

Galesburg Illinois, USA 20 B4

Galicia Spain 72 C1

Galilee, Sea of *see* Tiberias, Lake

Galle Sri Lanka 117 E4

Gallipoli Italy 77 E5

Gällivare Sweden 64 D3

Gallup New Mexico, USA 26 C2

Galveston Texas, USA 27 G4

Galway Ireland 69 A5

Gambia *Country* W Africa 52

Gäncä Azerbaijan
Rus. Gyandzha, *prev.*
Kirovabad, Yelisavetpol 97 G2

Gand *see* Gent

Gander Canada 19 H3

Gandía Spain 73 F3

Ganges *River* S Asia 114 D3

Ganges Delta *Wetlands*
Bangladesh/India 115 G4

Ganges Plain *Region* S Asia
104 C3

Gangtok India 115 G3

Ganzhou China 109 C6

Gao Mali 53 E3

Gar China 106 A4

Garagum *see* Karakumy

Garagum Kanaly *see*
Karakumskiy Kanal

Garda, Lago di *Lake* Italy 76 C2

Gardēz Afghanistan 103 E4

Garissa Kenya 55 C6

Garmo Peak *see* Communism
Peak

Garonne *River* France 71 B5

Garoowe Somalia 55 E5

Garoua Cameroon 56 B4

Gary Indiana, USA 20 B3

Gaspé Canada 19 F4

Gastonia North Carolina, USA
29 E2

Gävle Sweden 65 C6

Gaya India 115 F4

Gaza Gaza Strip 99 A6

Gazandzhyk Turkmenistan
var. Kazandzhik, *Turkm.*
Gazanjyk 102 B2

Gazanjyk *see* Gazandzhyk

Gaza Strip *Disputed territory*
SW Asia 99 A6

Gaziantep Turkey *prev.* Aintab
96 D4

Gazimağusa Cyprus
var. Famagusta
Gk. Ammochostos 96 C5

Gdańsk Poland *Ger.* Danzig
78 C2

Gdingen *see* Gdynia

Gdynia Poland *Ger.* Gdingen
78 C2

Gedaref Sudan 54 C4

Geelong Australia 130 B4

Gêkdepe Turkmenistan
prev. Geok-Tepe, *Turkm.*
Gökdepe 102 B3

Gelsenkirchen Germany 74 A4

Gemena Zaire 57 C5

Geneina Sudan 54 A4

General Eugenio A. Garay
Paraguay 42 A1

General Santos Philippines
121 F3

Geneva *see* Genève

Geneva, Lake *Lake*
France/Switzerland *Fr.* Lac
Léman, *var.* Le Léman,
Ger. Genfer See 71 D5 75 A8

Genève Switzerland
Eng. Geneva 75 A5

Genfer See *see* Geneva, Lake

Genk Belgium 67 D6

Genoa *see* Genova

Genova Italy *see* Genoa 76 B3

Genova, Golfo di *Sea feature*
Italy 76 B3

Gent Belgium *Fr.* Gand,
Eng. Ghent 67 B5

Geok-Tepe *see* Gêkdepe

Georgenburg *see* Jurbarkas

Georges Bank *Undersea feature*
Atlantic Ocean 21 H2

George Town *Capital of* Cayman
Islands 34 B3

Georgetown Gambia 52 B3

Georgetown *Capital of* Guyana
39 G2

George Town Malaysia 120 B3

Georgia *Country* SW Asia 97 F2

Georgia *State* USA 29 E3

Gera Germany 75 C5

Geraldton Australia 129 A5

Gereshk Afghanistan 102 D5

Germany *Country* W Europe
74-75

Getafe Spain 73 E3

Gettysburg Pennsylvania, USA
21 E4

Gevgelija Macedonia 81 E6

Ghadāmis Libya 51 E3

Ghana *Country* W Africa 53

Ghanzi Botswana 58 C3

Ghardaïa Algeria 50 D2

Gharyān Libya 51 F2

Ghāt Libya 51 F4

Ghaznī Afghanistan 103 E4

Ghent *see* Gent

Gibraltar *External territory* UK,
SW Europe 72 D5

Gibraltar, Strait of *Sea feature*
Atlantic Ocean/Mediterranean
Sea 72 D5

Gibson Desert *Desert region*
Australia 129 C5

Gijón Spain 72 D1

Gilbert Islands *Islands* Kiribati
127 E2

Gillette Wyoming, USA 22 C3

Girne Cyprus *var.* Kyrenia
96 C5

Girona Spain 73 G2

Gisborne New Zealand 131 H2

Giurgiu Romania 88 C5

Gjirokastër Albania 81 D6

Gjøvik Norway 65 B5

Glasgow Scotland, UK 68 C4

Glasgow Montana, USA 22 C1

Gleiwitz *see* Gliwice

Glendale Arizona, USA 26 B2

Glendive Montana, USA 22 D2

Gliwice Poland *Ger.* Gleiwitz
79 C5

Gloucester England, UK 69 D6

Glubokoye *see* Hlybokaye

Goa *State* India 116 C2

Gobi *Desert* China/Mongolia
106 D3

Godāveri *River* India 104 B3

Godoy Cruz Argentina 44 B4

Godthåb *see* Nuuk

Godwin Austin, Mount *see* K2

Goiânia Brazil 41 F4

Gökdepe *see* Gêkdepe

Golan Heights *Disputed territory*
SW Asia 98 B4

Gold Coast *Coastal region* Australia 130 D2

Goldingen *see* Kuldīga

Golmud China 106 D4

Goma Zaire 57 E6

Gomel' *see* Homyel'

Gómez Palacio Mexico 30 D2

Gonaïves Haiti 34 D3

Gonder Ethiopia 54 C4

Good Hope, Cape of *Coastal feature* South Africa 58 C5

Goondiwindi Australia 130 C2

Goose Lake *Lake* W USA 24 B4

Goré Chad 56 C4

Gorē Ethiopia 55 C5

Gorgān Iran 100 D3

Gorki *see* Horki

Gor'kiy *see* Nizhniy Novgorod

Gorlovka *see* Horlivka

Gorontalo Indonesia 121 E4

Górzow Wielkopolski Poland *Ger.* Landsberg 78 B3

Gospić Croatia 80 A3

Gostivar Macedonia 81 D5

Göteborg Sweden 65 B7

Gotland *Island* Sweden 65 C7

Gotō-rettō *Island group* Japan 111 A6

Göttingen Germany 74 B4

Gouda Netherlands 66 C4

Gough Island *External territory* UK, Atlantic Ocean 47 D6

Gouin, Réservoir *Reservoir* Canada 18 D4

Governador Valadares Brazil 41 G4 43 F1

Gozo *Island* Malta 77 C8

Gračanica Bosnia & Herzegovina 80 C3

Grafton Australia 130 D2

Graham Land *Region* Antarctica 132 B3

Grampian Mountains *Mountains* Scotland, UK 68 C3

Granada Nicaragua 32 D3

Granada Spain 73 E4

Gran Canaria *Island* Spain 50 A3

Gran Chaco *Region* C South America 36 C4

Grand Bahama *Island* Bahamas 34 C1

Grand Banks *Undersea feature* Atlantic Ocean 46 B3

Grand Canyon *Valley* SW USA 26 B1

Grande, Bahía *Sea feature* Argentina 37 C7

Grande, Rio *River* Brazil 42 D4 43 E1

Grande Comore *Island* Comoros 59 F2

Grande Prairie Canada 17 E5

Grand Erg Occidental *Desert region* Algeria 50 D2

Grand Erg Oriental *Desert region* Algeria/Tunisia 51 E3

Grand Falls Canada 19 H3

Grand Forks North Dakota, USA 23 E1

Grand Junction Colorado, USA 22 C4

Grand Rapids Michigan, USA 20 C3

Graudenz *see* Grudziądz

Graz Austria 75 E7

Great Abaco *Island* Bahamas 34 C1

Great Ararat *see* Ararat, Mount

Great Australian Bight *Sea feature* Australia 122 B4 129 D6

Great Bahama Bank *Undersea feature* Atlantic Ocean 34 C2

Great Barrier Reef *Coral reef* Coral Sea 122 C4

Great Basin *Region* USA 24 D4

Great Bear Lake *Lake* Canada 17 E3

Great Dividing Range *Mountain range* Australia 124 D3

Greater Antarctica *Region* Antarctica 133 F3

Greater Antilles *Island group* West Indies 34 C3

Great Exuma Island *Island* Bahamas 34 C2

Great Falls Montana, USA 22 B1

Great Inagua *Island* Bahamas 34 D2

Great Khingan Range *see* Da Hinggan Ling

Great Lakes, The *Lakes* N America *see* Erie, Huron, Michigan, Ontario, Superior 15 F3

Great Nicobar *Island* India 117 H3

Great Plain of China *Region* China 104 D2

Great Plains *Region* N America 14 D3

Great Rift Valley *Valley* E Africa/SW Asia 55 C6

Great Salt Lake *Salt lake* Utah, USA 22 B3

Great Sand Sea *Desert region* Egypt/Libya 51 H3

Great Sandy Desert *Desert* Australia 128 C4

Great Sandy Desert *Desert* Rub' al Khali

Great Slave Lake *Lake* Canada 17 F4

Great Victoria Desert *Desert* Australia 129 C5

Gredos, Sierra de *Mountains* Spain 72 D3

Greece *Country* SE Europe 84-85

Green Bay Wisconsin, USA 20 B2

Greenland *External territory* Denmark, Atlantic Ocean *var.* Grønland 62

Greenland Basin *Undersea feature* Atlantic Ocean 63 F2

Greenland Sea Atlantic Ocean 63 F2

Greenock Scotland, UK 68 C4

Greensboro North Carolina, USA 29 F1

Greenville South Carolina, USA 29 E2

Greifswald Germany 74 D2

Grenada *Country* West Indies 35 G5

Grenoble France 71 D5

Greymouth New Zealand 131 F3

Grimsby England, UK 69 E5

Grodno *see* Hrodna

Groningen Netherlands 66 E1

Grønland *see* Greenland

Grootfontein Namibia 58 C3

Grosseto Italy 76 B4

Grosskanizsa *see* Nagykanizsa

Groznyy Russian Federation 91 B7 94 A4

Grudziądz Poland *Ger.* Graudenz 78 C3

Grünberg in Schlesien *see* Zielona Góra

Guadalajara Mexico 30 D4

153

Hattiesburg Mississippi, USA 28 C3

Hat Yai Thailand 119 C7

Haugesund Norway 65 A6

Havana *Capital of* Cuba *Sp.* La Habana 34 B2

Havre Montana, USA 22 C1

Havre-Saint-Pierre Canada 19 F3

Hawaii *State* USA 123 E2

Hawaiian Islands *Islands* USA 93 H4

Hawlēr *see* Arbīl

Hawthorne Nevada, USA 25 C6

Hay River Canada 17 E4

Hays Kansas, USA 23 E4

Heard Island *Island* Indian Ocean 113 C7

Heerenveen Netherlands 66 D2

Heerlen Netherlands 67 D6

Ḥefa Israel *prev.* Haifa 99 A5

Hefei China 109 D5

Heidelberg Germany 75 B6

Heilbronn Germany 75 B6

Helena Montana, USA 22 B2

Helmand *River* Afghanistan 102 C5

Helmond Netherlands 67 D5

Helsingborg Sweden 65 B7

Helsingør Denmark 65 B7

Helsinki *Capital of* Finland 65 D6

Helwân Egypt 54 B1

Hengelo Netherlands 66 E3

Henzada Myanmar 118 A4

Herāt Afghanistan 102 C4

Hermansverk Norway 65 A5

Hermosillo Mexico 30 B2

Herning Denmark 65 A7

Hialeah Florida, USA 29 F5

Hiiumaa *Island* Estonia *Ger.* Dagden, *Swed.* Dagö 86 C2

Hildesheim Germany 74 B4

Hilla *see* Al Ḥillah

Hilversum Netherlands 66 C3

Himalayas *Mountain range* S Asia 104 B2

Himora Ethiopia 54 C4

Ḥimṣ Syria 98 B3

Hindu Kush *Mountain range* C Asia 103 E4

Hiroshima Japan 111 B5

Hitachi Japan 110 D4

Hjørring Denmark 65 A7

Hlybokaye Belarus *Rus.* Glubokoye 87 D5·

Hobart Tasmania 130 B5

Hobbs New Mexico, USA 5627 E3

Hô Chi Minh Vietnam *var.* Ho Chi Minh City, *prev.* Saigon 119 E6

Ho Chi Minh City *see* Hô Chi Minh

Hodeida *see* Al Ḥudaydah

Hoek van Holland Netherlands 66 B4

Hoggar *see* Ahaggar

Hohhot China 107 F3

Hokkaidō *Island* Japan 110 D2

Holguín Cuba 34 C2

Hollywood Florida, USA 29 F5

Holland *see* Netherlands

Holon Israel 99 A5

Holyhead Wales, UK 69 C5

Homyel' Belarus *Rus.* Gomel' 87 D7

Honduras *Country* Central America 32-33

Honduras, Gulf of *Sea feature* Caribbean Sea 32 C2

Hønefoss Norway 65 B6

Hông Gai Vietnam 118 E4

Hong Kong *External territory* UK, E Asia 109 C7

Hongze Hu *Lake* China 109 D5

Honiara *Capital of* Solomon Islands 126 C3

Honolulu Hawaii, USA 123 E2

Honshū *Island* Japan 110 D3

Honshu Ridge *Undersea feature* Pacific Ocean 105 F2

Hoorn Netherlands 66 C2

Hopa Turkey 97 F2

Hopedale Canada 19 F2

Hopkinsville Kentucky, USA 20 B5

Horki Belarus *Rus.* Gorki 87 E6

Horlivka Ukraine *Rus.* Gorlovka 88 G3

Horn, Cape *Coastal feature* Chile 45 C8

Horog *see* Khorog

Horsens Denmark 65 A7

Hotan China 106 B4

Hot Springs Arkansas, USA 28 B2

Hotspur Seamount *Undersea feature* Atlantic Ocean 41 H5 43 H1

Hô Thac Ba *Lake* Vietnam 118 D3

Houston Texas, USA 27 G4

Hovd Mongolia 106 C2

Hövsgöl Nuur *Lake* Mongolia 106 D1

Howe, Cape *Coastal feature* Australia 124 D4 130 C4

Hradec Králové Czech Republic *Ger.* Königgrätz 79 B5

Hrodna Belarus *Rus.* Grodno 87 B5

Huacho Peru 40 A3

Huainan China 109 D5

Huambo Angola 58 B2

Huancayo Peru 40 B4

Huang He *River* China *Eng.* Yellow River 104 D2 107 F4 108 C4

Huánuco Peru 40 B4

Huaraz Peru 40 B3

Huascarán *Peak* Peru 36 B3

Hubli India 116 C2

Hudson *River* NE USA 21 F3

Hudson Bay *Sea feature* Canada 15 E2

Hudson Strait *Sea feature* Canada 15 F2

Huê Vietnam 118 E4

Huehuetenango Guatemala 32 B2

Huelva Spain 72 C4

Huesca Spain 73 F2

Hughenden Australia 130 B1

Hull *see* Kingston upon Hull

Hulun Nur *Lake* China 107 F1·

Humboldt *River* W USA 25 C5

Hungarian Plain *Plain* C Europe 83 E1

Hungary *Country* C Europe 79

Huntington West Virginia, USA 20 D4

Huntsville Alabama, USA 28 D2

Hurghada Egypt 54 B2

Huron, Lake *Lake* Canada/USA 15 F3

155

Ittoqqortoormiit Greenland 13 B7 63 B3

Iturup *Island* Japan/Russian Federation (disputed) 110 E1

Ivanhoe Australia 130 B3

Ivano-Frankivs'k Ukraine 88 C2

Ivanovo Russian Federation 90 B4

Ivittuut Greenland 62 B4

Ivory Coast *Country* W Africa *Fr.* Côte d'Ivoire 52

Ivujivik Canada 18 D1

Iwaki Japan 110 D4

Izabal, Lago de *Lake* Guatemala 32 C2

Izhevsk Russian Federation 91 C5 94 B3

İzmir Turkey *prev.* Smyrna 96 A3

İzmit Turkey *var.* Kocaeli 96 B2

Izu-shotō *Island group* Japan 111 D6

J

Jabalpur India 114 E4

Jackson Mississippi, USA 28 C3

Jacksonville Florida, USA 29 E3

Jacksonville Texas, USA 27 G3

Jacmel Haiti 34 D3

Jaén Spain 73 E4

Jaffna Sri Lanka 117 E3

Jaipur India 114 D3

Jajce Bosnia & Herzegovina 80 B3

Jakarta *Capital of* Indonesia 120 C5

Jakobstad Finland 64 D4

Jakobstadt *see* Jēkabpils

Jalālābād Afghanistan 103 E4

Jalal-Abad *see* Dzhalal-Abad

Jalandhar India 114 D2

Jalapa Mexico 31 F4

Jamaame Somalia 55 D6

Jamaica *Country* West Indies 34

Jamālpur Bangladesh 115 G4

Jambi Indonesia 120 B4

James Bay *Sea feature* Canada 18 C3

Jammu *Disputed region* India/Pakistan 114 D2

Jāmnagar India 114 B4

Jan Mayen *External territory* Norway, Arctic Ocean 46 A2 63 F3

Japan *Country* E Asia 110-111

Japan, Sea of Pacific Ocean 93 F4 110 B3

Japan Trench *Undersea feature* Pacific Ocean 122 C2

Järvenpää Finland 65 D5

Jarvis Island *External territory* USA, Pacific Ocean 127 C2

Jaseur Seamount *Undersea feature* Atlantic Ocean 43 H2

Java *Island* Indonesia 120 C5

Java Sea Pacific Ocean *var.* Laut Jawa 112 D4

Java Trench *Undersea feature* Indian Ocean 112 D4

Jawa, Laut *see* Java Sea

Jayapura Indonesia 121 H4

Jedda *see* Jiddah

Jefferson City Missouri, USA 23 G4

Jēkabpils Latvia *Ger.* Jakobstadt 86 C4

Jelgava Latvia *Ger.* Mitau 86 C3

Jember Indonesia 120 D5

Jena Germany 75 C5

Jérémie Haiti 34 D3

Jerevan *see* Yerevan

Jerez de la Frontera Spain 72 D5

Jericho West Bank 99 B5

Jerid, Chott el *Salt lake* Africa 82 D4

Jersey *Island* Channel Islands 69 D8

Jerusalem *Capital of* Israel 99 B5

Jesenice Slovenia 80 A2

Jhelum Pakistan 114 C2

Jiamusi China 108 E2

Jibuti *see* Djibouti

Jiddah Saudi Arabia *Eng.* Jedda 101 A6

Jihlava Czech Republic *Ger.* Iglau 79 B5

Jilin China 108 D3

Jīma Ethiopia 55 C5

Jinan China 109 C4

Jingdezhen China 109 D6

Jining China 107 F2

Jinotega Nicaragua 32 D3

Jinsha Jiang *River* China 109 A6

Jisr ash Shughūr Syria 98 B2

Jixi China 108 E3

Jīzān Saudi Arabia 101 B6

João Pessoa Brazil 41 H3

Jodhpur India 114 C3

Joensuu Finland 65 E5

Johannesburg South Africa 58 D4

Johnson City Tennessee, USA 29 E1

Johor Bahru Malaysia 120 B3

Joinville Brazil 42 D3

Joliet Illinois, USA 20 B3

Jönköping Sweden 65 B7

Jonquière Canada 19 E4

Jordan *Country* SW Asia 98-99

Jordan *River* SW Asia 99 B5

Jos Nigeria 53 G4

Juan Fernandez, Islas *Islands* Chile 123 G4

Juàzeiro Brazil 41 G3

Juàzeiro do Norte Brazil 41 G3

Juba Sudan 55 B5

Júcar *River* Spain 73 E3

Judenburg Austria 75 D7

Juigalpa Nicaragua 32 D3

Juiz de Fora Brazil 41 G5 43 F2

Juneau Alaska, USA 16 D4

Junín Argentina 44 D4

Jura *Mountains* France/Switzerland 70 D4 75 A7

Jura *Island* Scotland, UK 68 B4

Jurbarkas Lithuania *Ger.* Jurburg, *var.* Georgenburg 86 B4

Jurburg *see* Jurbarkas

Juruá *River* Brazil/Peru 40 C2

Juticalpa Honduras 32 D2

Jutland *see* Jylland

Juventud, Isla de la *Island* Cuba 34 B2

Jylland *Peninsula* Denmark *Eng.* Jutland 65 A7

Jyväskylä Finland 65 D5

K

K2 *Peak* China/Pakistan *Eng.* Mount Godwin Austen 104 C2

Kaachka *see* Kaka

Kaakhka *see* Kaka

157

Kassa *see* Košice

Kassala Sudan 54 C4

Kassel Germany 74 B4

Kastamonu Turkey 96 C2

Katerini Greece 84 B4

Katha Myanmar 118 B2

Katherine Australia 128 D2

Kathmandu *Capital of* Nepal 115 F3

Katsina Nigeria 53 G3

Kauen *see* Kaunas

Kaunas Lithuania *Ger.* Kauen, *Pol.* Kowno, *Rus.* Kovno 86 B4

Kavadarci Macedonia 80 E5

Kavála Greece 84 C3

Kavaratti Island *Island* India 116 C3

Kawasaki Japan 111 D5

Kayan *River* Indonesia 120 D3

Kayes Mali 52 C3

Kayseri Turkey 96 D3

Kazakhskiy Melkosopochnik *see* Kazakh Upland

Kazakhstan *Country* C Asia 90

Kazakh Upland *Upland* Kazakhstan *var.* Kazakhskiy Melkosopochnik 92 D3

Kazan' Russian Federation 91 C5 94 B3

Kazandzhik *see* Gazandzhyk

Kazanlŭk Bulgaria 84 D2

Kéa *Island* Greece 85 C6

Kecskemét Hungary 79 D7

Kédainiai Lithuania 86 B4

Keetmanshoop Namibia 58 C4

Kefallonía *Island* Greece *Eng.* Cephalonia 85 A5

Keith Australia 130 B4

Kelang Malaysia 120 B3

Kelmé Lithuania 86 B4

Kelowna Canada 17 E5

Kemerovo Russian Federation 94 D4

Kemi Finland 64 D4

Kemi *River* Finland 64 D3

Kemijärvi Finland 64 D3

Kendari Indonesia 121 E4

Kenema Sierra Leone 52 C4

Këneurgench Turkmenistan *prev.* Kunya-Urgench, *Turkm.* Köneürgench 102 C2

Kénitra Morocco 50 C2

Kennewick Washington, USA 24 C2

Kenora Canada 18 A3

Kentucky *State* USA 20 C5

Kenya *Country* E Africa 55

Kenya, Mount *see* Kirinyaga

Kerala *State* India 116 D3

Kerbala *see* Karbalá'

Kerch Ukraine 89 G4

Kerguelen Islands *Island group* Indian Ocean 113 C6

Kerguelen Plateau *Undersea feature* Indian Ocean 113 C7

Kerki Turkmenistan 102 D3

Kérkira *see* Kérkyra

Kérkyra Greece 84 A4

Kérkyra *Island* Greece *prev.* Kérkira, *Eng.* Corfu 84 A4

Kermadec Islands *Island group* Pacific Ocean 125 F3

Kermadec Trench *Undersea feature* Pacific Ocean 122 D4

Kermān Iran *var.* Kirman 100 D4

Kermānshāh *see* Bākhtarān

Kerora Eritrea 54 C3

Kerulen *River* China/Mongolia 107 E2

Ketchikan Alaska, USA 16 D4

Key West Florida, USA 29 E5

Khabarovsk Russian Federation 95 G4

Khanka, Lake *Lake* China/Russian Federation 108 E3

Khankendy *see* Xankändi

Kharkiv Ukraine *Rus.* Khar'kov 89 G2

Khartoum *Capital of* Sudan *var.* Al Khurṭūm 54 B4

Khartoum North Sudan 54 B4

Khāsh Iran 100 E4

Khaskovo Bulgaria 84 D2

Khaydarkan Kyrgyzstan *var.* Khaydarken, Hajdarken 103 E2

Khaydarken *see* Khaydarkan

Kherson Ukraine 89 E4

Khíos *see* Chíos

Khmel 'nyts'kyy Ukraine 88 C2

Khodzhent *see* Khudzhand

Khojend *see* Khudzhand

Khokand *see* Kokand

Kholm Afghanistan 103 E3

Khon Kaen Thailand 118 C4

Khorog Tajikistan *var.* Horog 103 F3

Khorramshahr Iran *var.* Khūnīnshahr 100 C4

Khouribga Morocco 50 C2

Khudzhand Tajikistan *prev.* Leninabad, Khodzhent, Khojend 103 E2

Khulna Bangladesh 115 G4

Khūnīnshahr *see* Khorramshahr

Khvoy Iran 100 B2

Kičevo Macedonia 81 D5

Kiel Germany 74 B2

Kielce Poland 78 D4

Kiev *Capital of* Ukraine *Ukr.* Kyyiv 89 E2

Kiffa Mauritania 52 C3

Kigali *Capital of* Rwanda 55 B6

Kigoma Tanzania 55 B7

Kikládhes *see* Kyklades

Kikwit Zaire 57 C7

Kilimanjaro *Peak* Tanzania 49 D5

Kilkís Greece 84 B3

Killarney Ireland 69 A6

Kimberley South Africa 58 D4

Kimberley Plateau *Upland* Australia 128 C3

Kindia Guinea 52 C4

Kindu Zaire 57 D6

King Island *Island* Australia 130 B4

Kingissepp *see* Kuressaare

Kingman Reef *External territory* USA, Pacific Ocean 127 G2

Kingston Canada 18 C5

Kingston *Capital of* Jamaica 34 C3

Kingston upon Hull England, UK *var.* Hull 69 D5

Kingstown St Vincent & The Grenadines 34 G4

King William Island *Island* Canada 17 F3

Kinneret, Yam *see* Tiberias, Lake

Kinshasa *Capital of* Zaire *prev.* Léopoldville 57 B6

Kirghizia *see* Kyrgyzstan

Kirghiz Steppe *Plain* Kazakhstan 95 B4

Kotka Finland 65 E5
Kotlas NW Russia 90 C4
Kotto River C Africa 56 D4
Koudougou Burkina 53 E4
Kourou French Guiana 39 H2
Kousséri Cameroon 56 B3
Kouvola Finland 65 E5
Kovel' Ukraine 88 C1
Kovno see Kaunas
Kowno see Kaunas
Kozáni Greece 84 B4
Kozhikode see Calicut
Kra, Isthmus of Coastal feature Myanmar/Thailand 119 B6
Kragujevac Yugoslavia 80 D4
Krakatau Peak Indonesia 104 D5
Krakau see Kraków
Kraków Poland Eng. Cracow, Ger. Krakau 79 D5
Kraljevo Yugoslavia 80 D4
Kranj Slovenia 80 A2
Krasnodar Russian Federation 91 A6
Krasnovodsk see Turkmenbashy
Krasnoyarsk Russian Federation 94 D4
Krasnyy Luch Ukraine 89 G5
Kremenchuk Ukraine 89 F2
Kremenchuts'ke Vodoskhovyshche Reservoir Ukraine 89 E2
Krems an der Donau Austria 75 E6
Kretinga Lithuania Ger. Krottingen 86 B3
Kribi Cameroon 57 B5
Krichev see Krychaw
Krishna River India 116 C1
Kristiansand Norway 65 A6
Kristianstad Sweden 65 B7
Kríti Island Greece Eng. Crete 85 C7
Kritikó Pélagos see Crete, Sea of
Krivoy Rog see Kryvyy Rih
Krk Island Croatia 80 A3
Kroonstad South Africa 58 D4
Krottingen see Kretinga
Krung Thep see Bangkok
Kruševac Yugoslavia 81 D4
Krychaw Belarus Rus. Krichev 87 E6
Krym see Crimea

Kryvyy Rih Ukraine Rus. Krivoy Rog 89 E3
Kuala Lumpur Capital of Malaysia 120 B3
Kuala Terengganu Malaysia 120 B3
Kuantan Malaysia 120 B3
Kuba see Quba
Kuching Malaysia 120 C3
Kuçovë Albania prev. Qyteti Stalin 81 D6
Kuito Angola 58 C2
Kuldīga Latvia Ger. Goldingen 86 B3
Kullorsuaq Greenland 62 B3
Kulyab SW Tajikistan 103 E3
Kum see Qom
Kuma River Russian Federation 91 B7
Kumamoto Japan 111 A6
Kumanovo Macedonia 81 E5
Kumasi Ghana 53 E5
Kumayri see Gyumri 97 F2
Kumbo Cameroon 56 B4
Kumon Range Mountain range Myanmar 118 B1
Kunashir Island Japan/Russian Federation (disputed) 110 E1
Kunduz var. Kondūz, Qondūz, Kondoz 103 E3
Kunja-Urgenč see Këneurgench
Kunlun Mountains see Kunlun Shan
Kunlun Shan Mountain range China Eng. Kunlun Mountains 104 C2 106 B4
Kunming China 109 A6
Kununurra Australia 128 D3
Kupang Indonesia 120 E5
Kür see Kura
Kura River Azerbaijan/Georgia Az. Kür 96 G2
Kurashiki Japan 111 B5
Küre Dağları Mountains Turkey 96 C2
Kuressaare Estonia prev. Kingissepp, Ger. Arensburg 86 C2
Kurgan-Tyube Tajikistan 103 E3
Kurile Islands Islands Pacific Ocean 105 F1
Kurile Trench Undersea feature Pacific Ocean 122 C2

Kurmuk Sudan 54 C4
Kurnool India 116 D2
Kuršėnai Lithuania 86 B4
Kushiro Japan 110 E2
Kushka see Gushgy
Kustanay Kazakhstan 94 C4
Kütahya Turkey prev. Kutaiah 96 B3
Kutaiah see Kütahya
K'ut'aisi Georgia 97 F2
Kutch, Rann of see Kachch, Rann of
Kuujjuaq Canada 19 E2
Kuujjuarapik Canada 18 D2
Kuusamo Finland 64 E4
Kuwait Country SW Asia 100 C4
Kuwait City Capital of Kuwait 100 C4
Kuytun China 106 B3
Kwangju South Korea 109 E5
Kwango River Zaire 57 C7
Kykládes Island group Greece prev. Kikládhes, Eng. Cyclades 85 D6
Kyrenia see Girne
Kyrgyzstan Country C Asia var. Kirghizia 103
Kýthira Island Greece 85 B6
Kyushu-Palau Ridge Undersea feature Pacific Ocean 111 B7 121 G1
Kyyiv see Kiev
Kyzyl Kum Desert Kazakhstan/Uzbekistan var. Kizil Kum, Uzb. Qizilqum 92 C3
Kyōto Japan 111 C5
Kyūshū Island Japan 111 B6
Kzyl-Orda Kazakhstan 94 B5

L

Laâyoune Western Sahara 50 B3
Labé Guinea 52 C4
Laborca see Laborec
Laborec River Slovakia Hung. Laborca 79 E5
Labrador Region Canada 19 F2
Labrador Basin Undersea feature Atlantic Ocean 15 G2 19 H1
Labrador City Canada 19 E3
Labrador Sea Atlantic Ocean 62 B5

Laccadive Islands *see* Lakshadweep

La Ceiba Honduras 32 D2

La Coruña *see* A Coruña

La Crosse Wisconsin, USA 20 A2

Ladoga, Lake *see* Ladozhskoye Ozero

Ladozhskoye Ozero *Lake* Russian Federation *Eng.* Lake Ladoga 90 B3

Lae Papua New Guinea 126 B3

La Esperanza Honduras 32 C2

Lafayette Louisiana, USA 28 B3

Lågen *River* Norway 65 B5

Laghouat Algeria 50 D2

Lagos Nigeria 53 F5

Lagos Portugal 72 C4

La Grande Oregon, USA 24 C3

La Habana *see* Havana

Lahore Pakistan 114 C2

Laï Chad 56 C4

Laila *see* Laylá

Lajes Brazil 42 D3

Lake District *Region* England, UK 69 C5

Lakewood Colorado, USA 22 D4

Lakshadweep *Island group* India *Eng.* Laccadive Islands 116 B2

La Ligua Chile 44 B4

La Louvière Belgium 67 B6

Lambaré Paraguay 42 B3

Lambaréné Gabon 57 B6

Lambert Glacier *Ice feature* Antarctica 133 G2

Lamía Greece 85 B5

Lampedusa *Island* Italy 77 B8

Lampione *Island* Italy 77 B8

Lancaster England, UK 69 D5

Lancaster California, USA 25 C7

Lancaster Sound *Sea feature* Canada 17 G2

Landsberg *see* Gorzów Wielkopolski

Land's End *Coastal feature* England, UK 69 B7

Lang Sơn Vietnam 118 D3

Länkäran Azerbaijan *Rus.* Lenkoran' 97 H3

Lansing Michigan, USA 20 C3

Lanzarote *Island* Spain 50 B3

Lanzhou China 108 B4

Laon France 70 D3

La Oroya Peru 40 B3

Laos *Country* SE Asia 118

La Palma *Island* Spain 50 A3

La Paz *Capital* of Bolivia 40 C4

La Paz Mexico 30 B3

La Pérouse Strait *Sea feature* Japan 110 D1

Lapland *Region* N Europe 64 C3

La Plata Argentina 44 D4

Lappeenranta Finland 65 E5

Laptev Sea *see* Laptevykh, More

Laptevykh, More Arctic Ocean *Eng.* Laptev Sea 12 E3 95 F2

L'Aquila Italy 76 C4

Laramie Wyoming, USA 22 C4

Laredo Texas, USA 27 F5

La Rioja Argentina 44 C3

Lárisa Greece 84 B4

Lārkāna Pakistan 114 B3

Larnaca Cyprus *var.* Larnaka, Larnax 96 C5

Larnaka *see* Larnaca

Larnax *see* Larnaca

La Rochelle France 70 B4

La Roche-sur-Yon France 70 B4

La Romana Dominican Republic 34 E3

Las Cruces New Mexico, USA 26 D3

La Serena Chile 44 B3

La Spezia Italy 76 B3

Las Piedras Uruguay 42 C5

Las Tablas Panama 33 F5

Las Vegas Nevada, USA 25 D7

Latakia *see* Al Lādhiqīyah

Latvia *Country* NE Europe 84

Launceston Tasmania 130 B6

Laurentian Basin *see* Canada Basin

Laurentian Plateau *Upland* Canada 15 F3

Lausanne Switzerland 73 A7

Laval France 70 B3

Lawton Oklahoma, USA 27 F2

Laylá Saudi Arabia 101 C5

Lebanon *Country* SW Asia 98-99

Lebu Chile 45 B5

Lecce Italy 77 E5

Leduc Canada 17 E5

Leeds England, UK 69 D5

Leeuwarden Netherlands 66 D1

Leeuwin, Cape *Coastal feature* Australia 129 B6

Leeward Islands *Island group* West Indies 35 G3

Lefkáda *Island* Greece *prev.* Levkás 85 A5

Lefkoşa *see* Nicosia

Lefkosia *see* Nicosia

Legaspi Philippines 120 E2

Legnica Poland *Ger.* Liegnitz 78 B4

Le Havre France 70 B3

Leicester England, UK 69 D6

Leiden Netherlands 66 C3

Leipzig Germany 74 C4

Leivádia Greece 85 B5

Leizhou Bandao *Peninsula* China 109 C7

Lek *River* Netherlands 66 C4

Le Léman *see* Geneva, Lake

Lelystad Netherlands 66 D3

Léman, Lac *see* Geneva, Lake

Le Mans France 70 B3

Lemesos *see* Limassol

Lemnos *see* Límnos

Lena *River* Russian Federation 95 F3

Leninabad *see* Khudzhand

Leninakan *see* Gyumri

Leningrad *see* St Petersburg

Leninsk *see* Chardzhev

Lenkoran' *see* Länkäran

León Mexico 31 E4

León Nicaragua 32 C3

León Spain 72 D2

Léopoldville *see* Kinshasa

Lepel' *see* Lyepyel'

Le Puy France 71 C5

Lérida *see* Lleida

Lerwick Scotland, UK 68 D1

Lesbos *see* Lésvos

Leskovac Yugoslavia 80 E4

Lesotho *Country* southern Africa 58

Lesser Antarctica *Region* Antarctica 134 C2

Lesser Antilles *Island group* West Indies 35 G4

Lésvos *Island* Greece *Eng.* Lesbos 83 F3 85 D4

Lethbridge Canada 17 F5
Leti, Kepulauan *Island group* Indonesia 121 F5
Leuven Belgium 67 C6
Leverkusen Germany 75 A5
Levkás *see* Lefkáda
Lewis *Island* Scotland, UK 68 B2
Lewiston Idaho, USA 24 C2
Lewiston Maine, USA 21 G2
Lexington Kentucky, USA 20 C5
Leyte *Island* Philippines 121 E2
Lezhë Albania 81 D5
Lhasa China 106 C5
Liangyungang China 109 D5
Liaoyuan China 108 D3
Libau *see* Liepāja
Liberec Czech Republic *Ger.* Reichenberg 78 B4
Liberia *Country* W Africa 52
Liberia Costa Rica 32 D4
Libreville *Capital of* Gabon 57 A5
Libya *Country* N Africa 51
Libyan Desert *Desert* N Africa 48 C3
Liechtenstein *Country* C Europe 75 B7
Liège Belgium 67 D6
Liegnitz *see* Legnica
Lienz Austria 75 D7
Liepāja Latvia *Ger.* Libau 86 B3
Liffey *River* Ireland 69 B5
Ligurian Sea Mediterranean Sea 71 E6
Likasi Zaire 57 E8
Lille France 70 C2
Lillehammer Norway 65 B5
Lilongwe *Capital of* Malawi 59 E2
Lima *Capital of* Peru 40 B4
Lima Ohio, USA 20 C4
Limassol Cyprus *var.* Lemesos 96 C5
Limerick Ireland 69 A6
Límnos *Island* Greece *var.* Lemnos 84 C4
Limoges France 70 C5
Limón Costa Rica 33 E4
Limpopo *River* southern Africa 58 D3
Linares Chile 44 B4
Linares Spain 73 E4

Lincoln England, UK 69 D5
Lincoln Nebraska, USA 23 F4
Lincoln Sea Arctic Ocean 62 B1
Linden Guyana 39 G2
Lindi *River* Zaire 55 C8
Line Islands *Island group* Kiribati 127 H3
Lingga, Kepulauan *Island group* Indonesia 120 B4
Linköping Sweden 65 C6
Linosa *Island* Italy 77 C8
Linz Austria 75 D6
Lion, Golfe du *Sea feature* Mediterranean Sea 82 C2
Lipari *Island* Italy 77 D6
Lipari Islands *see* Isole Eolie
Lira Uganda 55 B6
Lisbon *Capital of* Portugal *Port.* Lisboa 72 B4
Litang China 109 A5
Litani *River* SW Asia 89 B4
Lithuania *Country* E Europe 86-87
Little Andaman *Island* India 117 G2
Little Minch *Sea feature* Scotland, UK 68 B3
Little Rock Arkansas, USA 28 B2
Liuzhou China 109 B7
Liverpool England, UK 69 D5
Livingston, Lake *Lake* Texas, USA 27 H3
Livingstone Zambia 58 D3
Livno Bosnia & Herzegovina 80 B4
Livorno Italy 76 B3
Ljubljana *Capital of* Slovenia 80 A2
Ljusnan *River* Sweden 65 B5
Llanos *Region* Colombia/Venezuela 39 E2
Lleida Spain *Cast.* Lérida 73 F2
Lobatse Botswana 58 D4
Lobito Angola 58 B2
Locarno Switzerland 75 B8
Lodja Zaire 57 D6
Lódź Poland *Rus.* Lodz 78 D4
Lofoten *Island group* Norway 64 B3
Logan, Mount *Peak* Canada 14 C2

Logroño Spain 73 E2
Loire *River* France 70 B4
Loja Ecuador 38 A5
Lokitaung Kenya 55 C5
Loksa Estonia *Ger.* Loxa 86 D2
Lombok *Island* Indonesia 120 D5
Lomé *Capital of* Togo 53 F5
Lomond, Loch *Lake* Scotland, UK 68 C4
Lomonosov Ridge *Undersea feature* Arctic Ocean *var.* Harris Ridge 12 D4
London Canada 18 C5
London *Capital of* UK 69 E6
Londonderry Northern Ireland, UK 68 B4
Londonderry, Cape *Coastal feature* Australia 124 B2 128 C2
Londrina Brazil 42 D2
Long Beach California, USA 25 C8
Long Island *Island* Bahamas 34 D2
Long Island *Island* NE USA 21 G3
Longreach Australia 126 B5
Longview Texas, USA 27 G3
Longview Washington, USA 24 B2
Longyearbyen Svalbard 63 G2
Lop Nur *Lake* China 106 C3
Lorca Spain 73 F4
Lord Howe Rise *Undersea feature* Pacific Ocean 122 C4
Lorient France 70 A3
Los Alamos New Mexico, USA 26 D2
Los Angeles California, USA 25 C8
Loslau *see* Wodzisław Śląski
Los Mochis Mexico 30 C3
Losonc *see* Lučenec
Losontz *see* Lučenec
Lot *River* France 71 B5
Louangphrabang Laos 118 C3
Loubomo Congo 57 B6
Louisiana *State* USA 28 B3
Louisville Kentucky, USA 20 C5
Lovech Bulgaria 84 C2
Lower California *see* Baja California

Loxa *see* Loksa
Loyauté, Îles *Island group* New Caledonia 126 D5
Loznica Yugoslavia 80 C3
Luanda *Capital of* Angola 58 B1
Luanshya Zambia 58 D2
Lubānas Ezers *Lake* Latvia 86 D4
Lubango Angola 58 B2
Lubbock Texas, USA 27 E2
Lübeck Germany 74 C3
Lublin Poland *Rus.* Lyublin 78 E4
Lubny Ukraine 89 F2
Lubumbashi Zaire 57 E8
Lucapa Angola 58 C1
Lucena Philippines 120 E1
Lučenec Slovakia *Hung.* Losonc, *Ger.* Losontz 79 D6
Lucerne *see* Luzern
Lucknow India 115 E3
Lüderitz Namibia 58 B4
Ludhiāna India 114 D2
Lugano Switzerland 75 B8
Lugo Spain 72 C1
Luhans'k Ukraine 89 H3
Luleå Sweden 64 D4
Lumsden New Zealand 131 F5
Luninyets Belarus 97 C6
Lusaka *Capital of* Zambia 58 D2
Lushnjë Albania 81 D6
Lūt, Baḥrat *see* Dead Sea
Luts'k Ukraine 88 C1
Lutzow-Holm Bay *Sea feature* Antarctica 133 F1
Luxembourg *Country* W Europe 67 D8
Luxembourg *Capital of* Luxembourg 67 D8
Luxor Egypt 54 B2
Luzern Switzerland *Fr.* Lucerne 75 B7
Luzon *Island* Philippines 121 E1
Luzon Strait *Sea feature* Philippines/Taiwan 105 E3
L'viv Ukraine *Rus.* L'vov 88 B2
L'vov *see* L'viv
Lyepyel' Belarus *Rus.* Lepel' 87 D7
Lyon France 71 D5
Lyublin *see* Lublin

M

Ma'ān Jordan 99 B6
Maas *River* W Europe *var.* Meuse 66 D4
Maastricht Netherlands 67 D6
Macao *External territory* Portugal, E Asia *var.* Macau 109 C7
Macapá Brazil 41 F1
Macau *see* Macao
Macdonald Islands *Islands* Indian Ocean 113 B7
Macdonnell Ranges *Mountains* Australia 128 D4
Macedonia *Country* SE Europe officially Former Yugoslav Republic of Macedonia, *abbrev.* FYR Macedonia 81
Maceió Brazil 41 H3
Machakos Kenya 55 C6
Machala Ecuador 38 A5
Mackay Australia 126 B5 130 C1
Mackay, Lake *Lake* Australia 128 D4
Mackenzie *River* Canada 17 E4
Mackenzie Bay *Sea feature* Atlantic Ocean 133 G2
Mâcon France 70 D5
Macon Georgia, USA 29 E2
Madagascar *Country* Indian Ocean 59
Madagascar Basin *Undersea feature* Indian Ocean 113 B5
Madagascar Ridge *Undersea feature* Indian Ocean 113 A5
Madang Papua New Guinea 126 B3
Madeira *River* Bolivia/Brazil 40 D2
Madeira *Island group* Portugal 50 A2
Madhya Pradesh *State* India 115 E4
Madison Wisconsin, USA 20 B3
Madona Latvia *Ger.* Modohn 86 D3
Madras India 117 E2
Madre de Dios *River* Bolivia/Peru 40 C3
Madrid *Capital of* Spain 73 E3
Madurai India 116 D3

Magadan Russian Federation 95 G3
Magallanes *see* Punta Arenas
Magallanes, Estrecho de *see* Magellan, Strait of
Magdalena *River* Colombia 38 B2
Magdeburg Germany 74 C4
Magellan, Strait of *Sea feature* S South America *Sp.* Estrecho de Magallanes 37 B7
Maggiore, Lake *Lake* Italy/Switzerland 75 B8
Mahajanga Madagascar 59 G2
Mahalapye Botswana 58 D3
Mahanādi *River* India 115 F5
Mahārāshtra *State* India 114 D5
Mahé *Island* Seychelles 59 H1
Mahilyow Belarus *Rus.* Mogilëv 87 E6
Mährisch-Ostrau *see* Ostrava
Maicao Colombia 38 C1
Maiduguri Nigeria 53 H4
Maimana *see* Meymaneh
Maine *State* USA 21 G1
Mainz Germany 75 B5
Maiquetía Venezuela 38 D1
Maíz, Islas del *Islands* Nicaragua 33 E3 34 B5
Majorca *see* Mallorca
Majuro *Island* Marshall Islands 126 D1
Makarska Croatia 80 B4
Makeni Sierra Leone 52 C4
Makeyevka *see* Makiyivka
Makgadikgadi *Salt pan* Botswana 58 D3
Makhachkala Russian Federation 91 B7 94 A4
Makiyivka Ukraine *Rus.* Makeyevka 89 G5
Makkah Saudi Arabia *Eng.* Mecca 101 A5
Makkovik Canada 19 G2
Makurdi Nigeria 53 G4
Malabo *Capital of* Equatorial Guinea 57 A5
Malacca *see* Melaka
Malacca, Strait of *Sea feature* Indonesia/Malaysia 104 C4 119 C8

Maladzyechna Belarus
Rus. Molodechno,
Pol. Molodeczno 87 C5

Málaga Spain 72 E5

Malakal Sudan 55 B5

Malang Indonesia 120 D5

Malanje Angola 58 B1

Malatya Turkey 97 E3

Malawi *Country* southern
Africa 59

Malay Peninsula *Peninsula*
Malaysia / Thailand 119 D8

Malaysia *Country* Asia 120

Maldive Ridge *Undersea feature*
Indian Ocean 112 C4

Maldives *Country* Indian Ocean
116

Male' *Capital of* Maldives
116 C4

Mali *Country* W Africa 53

Malindi Kenya 55 C7

Mallorca *Island* Spain
Eng. Majorca 73 H3

Malmö Sweden 65 B5

Malta *Country* Mediterranean
Sea 77 C8

Malta Montana, USA 22 C1

Malta Channel *Sea feature*
Mediterranean Sea 77 C7

Maluku *Island group* Indonesia
var. Moluccas 105 E4 121 F4

Maluku, Laut Pacific Ocean
Eng. Molucca Sea 121 F4

Māmallapuram India 117 E2

Mamberamo *River* Indonesia
121 H4

Mamoudzou *Capital of* Mayotte
59 G2

Man Ivory Coast 52 D4

Man, Isle of *Island* UK 69 C5

Manado Indonesia 120 F3

Managua *Capital of* Nicaragua
32 D3

Manama *Capital of* Bahrain
Ar. Al Manāmah 101 C5

Mananjary Madagascar 59 G3

Manaus Brazil 40 D2

Manchester England, UK 69 D5

Manchester New Hampshire,
USA 21 G2

Manchuria *Region* China 108 D3

Manchurian Plain *Plain* E Asia
105 E1

Mandalay Myanmar 118 B3

Mangalia Romania 88 D5

Mangalore India 116 C2

Manguéni, Plateau du *Upland*
Niger 53 H2

Manicouagan, Réservoir
Reservoir Canada 19 E3

Manila *Capital of* Philippines
120 E1

Manisa Turkey *prev.* Saruhan
96 A3

Manitoba *Province* Canada
17 G4

Manizales Colombia 38 B3

Manjimup Australia 129 B6

Manlitsoq Greenland 62 B4

Mannar Sri Lanka 117 E3

Mannar, Gulf of *Sea feature*
Indian Ocean 116 D3

Mannheim Germany 75 B5

Mannu *River* Italy 77 A5

Manono Zaire 57 E7

Mansel Island Canada
18 C1

Manta Ecuador 38 A4

Mantes-la-Jolie France 70 C3

Mantova Italy *Eng.* Mantua
76 B2

Mantua *see* Mantova

Manzhouli China 107 F1

Mao Chad 56 B3

Maoke, Pegunungan *Mountains*
Indonesia 121 H4

Maputo *Capital of* Mozambique
59 E4

Mar, Serra do *Mountains* Brazil
36 D4

Maracaibo Venezuela 38 C1

Maracaibo, Lago de *Inlet*
Venezuela 38 C1

Maracay Venezuela 38 D1

Maradi Niger 53 G3

Marajó, Ilha de *Island* Brazil
41 F2

Marañón *River* Peru 40 B2

Maraş *see* Kahramanmaraş

Marash *see* Kahramanmaraş

Marbella Spain 72 D5

Mar Chiquita, Laguna *Salt lake*
Argentina 44 D3

Mardān Pakistan 114 C1

Mar del Plata Argentina 45 D5

Mardin Turkey 97 E4

Margarita, Isla de *Island*
Venezuela 35 F3 39 E1

Mārgow, Dasht-e- *Desert*
Afghanistan 112 C2

Mariana Trench *Undersea feature*
Pacific Ocean 122 C2

Marías, Islas *Islands* Mexico
30 C4

Maribor Slovenia 80 B2

Marie Byrd Land *Region*
Antarctica 132 C3

Mariehamn Finland 65 D6

Marijampolė Lithuania
prev. Kapsukas 86 B4

Marília Brazil 41 F5 42 D2

Maringá Brazil 42 D2

Marion, Lake *Lake* South
Carolina, USA 29 F2

Mariscal Estigarribia Paraguay
42 B2

Maritsa *River* SE Europe 84 D3

Mariupol' Ukraine
prev. Shdanov 89 G4

Marka Somalia 55 D6

Markham, Mount *Peak*
Antarctica 132 B4

Marmara, Sea of *see* Marmara
Denizi

Marmara Denizi Turkey
Eng. Sea of Marmara 96 B2

Marne *River* France 70 D3

Maroua Cameroon 56 B3

Marowijne *River* French
Guiana / Suriname 39 H3

Marquesas Islands *Island group*
French Polynesia *Fr.* Îles
Marquises 125 H2

Marquette Michigan, USA 20 B1

Marquisas, Îles *see* Marquesas
Islands

Marrakech Morocco
Eng. Marrakesh 50 B2

Marsala Italy 77 C7

Marseille France 71 D6

Marshall Islands *Country* Pacific
Ocean 126-127

Marsh Island *Island* Louisiana,
USA 29 B4

Martin Slovakia *prev.* Turčiansky
Svätý Martin,
Ger. Sankt Martin,
Hung. Túróczszentmárton
79 C5

Martinique *External territory*
France, West Indies 35

165

Mary Turkmenistan *prev.* Merv 102 C3

Maryland *State* USA 21 F4

Mascarene Islands *Island group* Indian Ocean 59 H3

Mascarene Plateau *Undersea feature* Indian Ocean 113 B5

Maseru *Capital of* Lesotho 58 D4

Mashhad Iran *var.* Meshed 100 E3

Masindi Uganda 55 B6

Mason City Iowa, USA 23 F3

Masqaṭ *see* Muscat

Massachusetts *State* USA 21 G3

Massawa Eritrea 54 C4

Massif Central France 71 C5

Massoukou Gabon 57 B6

Masterton New Zealand 131 G3

Matadi Zaire 57 B7

Matagalpa Nicaragua 32 D3

Matamoros Mexico 31 E2

Matanzas Cuba 34 B2

Matara Sri Lanka 117 E4

Mataró Spain 73 G2

Mato Grosso, Planalto de *Upland* Brazil 41 E3

Matosinhos Portugal 72 C2

Matrûh Egypt 54 B1

Matsue Japan 111 B5

Matsuyama Japan 111 B5

Maturín Venezuela 39 E1

Maun Botswana 58 D3

Mauritania *Country* W Africa 52

Mauritius *Country* Indian Ocean 59 H3

Mayaguana Island Bahamas 34 D2

Mayotte *External territory* France, Indian Ocean 59 G2

Mayyit, Al Baḥr al *see* Dead Sea

Mazār-e Sharīf Afghanistan 102 D3

Mazatenango Guatemala 32 B2

Mazatlán Mexico 30 C3

Mažeikiai Lithuania 86 B3

Mazury *Region* Poland 78 D3

Mazyr Belarus *Rus.* Mozyr' 87 D7

Mbabane *Capital of* Swaziland 59 E4

Mbala Zambia 59 E1

Mbale Uganda 55 C6

Mbandaka Zaire 57 C5

Mbeya Tanzania 55 B8

Mbuji-Mayi Zaire 57 D7

McKinley, Mount *see* Denali

McMurdo Sound *Sea feature* Antarctica 133 B5

Mead, Lake *Lake* SW USA 25 D7 26 A1

Mecca *see* Makkah

Mechelen Belgium 67 C5

Medan Indonesia 120 A3

Medellín Colombia 38 B2

Médenine Tunisia 51 F2

Medford Oregon, USA 24 B4

Medina *see* Al Madīnah

Mediterranean Sea Atlantic Ocean 82-83

Meekatharra Australia 129 B5

Meerut India 114 D3

Mek'elē Ethiopia 54 C4

Meknès Morocco 50 C2

Mekong *River* SE Asia 104 D3

Mekong Delta *Wetlands* Vietnam 119 E6

Melaka Malaysia *prev.* Malacca 120 B3

Melanesia *Region* Pacific Ocean 124-125 126-127

Melbourne Australia 130 B4

Melbourne Florida, USA 29 F4

Melilla *External territory* Spain, N Africa 50 C1

Melitopol' Ukraine 89 F4

Melo Uruguay 42 C4

Melville Island *Island* Australia 128 D2

Melville Island *Island* Canada 17 E2

Memel *see* Klaipėda

Memel *see* Neman

Memphis Tennessee, USA 28 C2

Mende France 71 C6

Mendi Papua New Guinea 126 B3

Mendoza Argentina 44 B4

Menongue Angola 58 C2

Menorca Island Spain *Eng.* Minorca 73 H3

Mentawai, Kepulauan *Island group* Indonesia 120 A4

Meppel Netherlands 66 D2

Merced California, USA 25 B6

Mercedario *Peak* Argentina 37 B5

Mercedes Argentina 44 C4

Mercedes Uruguay 42 B5

Mergui Myanmar 119 B5

Mergui Archipelago *Island chain* Myanmar 119 B6

Mérida Mexico 31 H3

Mérida Spain 72 C4

Mérida Venezuela 38 C2

Meridian Mississippi, USA 28 C3

Merredin Australia 129 B6

Mersin Turkey *var.* İçel 96 C4

Meru Kenya 55 C5

Merv *see* Mary

Mesa Arizona, USA 26 B2

Meshed *see* Mashhad

Messina Italy 77 D6

Messina, Stretto di *Sea feature* Ionian Sea/Tyrrhenian Sea 77 D7

Mesters Vig Greenland 62 D3

Mestre Italy 76 C2

Meta *River* Colombia/Venezuela 38 C2

Metković Croatia 80 C4

Metz France 70 D3

Meuse *River* W Europe *var.* Maas 70 D3

Mexicali Mexico 30 A1

Mexicana, Altiplanicie *see* Mexico, Plateau of

Mexico *Country* North America 30-31

México, Golfo de *see* Mexico, Gulf of

Mexico, Gulf of *Sea feature* Atlantic Ocean/Caribbean Sea 46 A4

Mexico, Plateau of *Upland* Mexico *Sp.* Altiplanicie Mexicana 14 D4

Mexico City *Capital of* Mexico *Sp.* Ciudad de México 31 E4

Meymaneh Afghanistan *var.* Maimana 102 D4

Mezen' *River* Russian Federation 90 D3

Miami Florida, USA 29 F5

Michigan *State* USA 20 C2

Michigan, Lake *Lake* USA 20 C2
Micronesia *Country* Pacific Ocean 126
Micronesia *Region* Pacific Ocean 126-127
Mid Atlantic Ridge *Undersea feature* Atlantic Ocean 46 B4
Middelburg South Africa 58 D5
Middle America Trench *Undersea feature* Pacific Ocean 36 A1
Middle Andaman *Island* India 117 G2
Middlesbrough England, UK 69 D5
Mid-Indian Ridge *Undersea feature* Indian Ocean 113 C5
Midland Texas, USA 27 E2
Mikhaylovka Russian Federation 91 B6
Mikkeli Finland 65 E5
Míkonos *Island* Greece 85 D6
Milagro Ecuador 38 A4
Milan *see* Milano
Milano Italy *Eng.* Milan 76 B2
Mildura Australia 130 B3
Miles Australia 130 C2
Miles City Montana, USA 22 C2
Milford Haven Wales, UK 69 C6
Milford Sound New Zealand 131 E4
Mílos *Island* Greece 85 C6
Milparinka Australia 130 B2
Milwaukee Wisconsin, USA 20 B3
Minatitlán Mexico 31 G4
Mindanao *Island* Philippines 121 F2
Mindoro *Island* Philippines 121 E2
Mindoro Strait *Sea feature* South China Sea/Sulu Sea 121 E2
Mingãçevir Azerbaijan *Rus.* Mingechaur 97 G2
Mingechaur *see* Mingãçevir
Minho *River* Portugal/Spain *Sp.* Miño 72 C2
Minicoy Island *Island* India 116 C3
Minneapolis Minnesota, USA 23 F2
Minnesota *State* USA 23 F1
Miño *River* Portugal/Spain *Port.* Minho 72 C1

Minorca *see* Menorca
Minot North Dakota, USA 22 D1
Minsk *Capital of* Belarus 87 C5
Minto, Lake *Lake* Canada 18 D2
Miranda de Ebro Spain 73 E2
Mirim, Lake *Lagoon* Brazil/Uruguay *var.* Mirim Lagoon 42 C5
Mirtóo Pelagos *Sea feature* Mediterranean Sea 85 C6
Miskitos Cayos *Islands* Nicaragua 33 E2
Miskolc Hungary 79 D6
Mişrātah Libya 51 F2
Mississippi *State* USA 28 C2
Mississippi *River* USA 15 E4
Mississippi Delta *Wetlands* USA 15 E4
Missoula Montana, USA 22 B2
Missouri *State* USA 23 G5
Missouri *River* USA 23 G4
Mistassini, Lake *Lake* Canada 18 D3
Mitau *see* Jelgava
Mitchell South Dakota, USA 23 E3
Mitilíni Greece 84 D4
Mito Japan 110 D4
Miyazaki Japan 111 B6
Mjøsa *Lake* Norway 65 B5
Mljet *Island* Croatia 81 C5
Mmabatho South Africa 58 D4
Mo Norway 64 C3
Mobile Alabama, USA 28 C3
Moçambique Mozambique 59 F2
Mocímboa da Praia Mozambique 59 F2
Mocoa Colombia 38 B4
Mocuba Mozambique 59 F2
Modena Italy 76 B3
Modesto California, USA 25 B6
Mödling Austria 75 E6
Modohn *see* Madona
Modriča Bosnia & Herzegovina 80 C3
Mogadiscio *see* Mogadishu
Mogadishu *Capital of* Somalia *Som.* Muqdisho, *It.* Mogadiscio 55 D6
Mogilëv *see* Mahilyow

Mohéli *Island* Comoros 59 F2
Mohns Ridge *Undersea feature* Greenland Sea 63 F3
Mojave California, USA 25 C7
Mojave Desert *Desert* W USA 25 D7
Moldavia *see* Moldova
Molde Norway 65 A5
Moldova *Country* E Europe *var.* Moldavia 88
Molodechno *see* Maladzyechna
Molodeczno *see* Maladzyechna
Molotov *see* Perm'
Moluccas *see* Maluku
Molucca Sea *see* Maluku, Laut
Mombasa Kenya 55 C7
Monaco *Country* W Europe 71 E6
Monastir Tunisia 51 F1
Monclova Mexico 31 E2
Moncton Canada 19 F4
Mongo Chad 56 C3
Mongolia *Country* NE Asia 106-107
Monroe Louisiana, USA 28 B2
Monrovia *Capital of* Liberia 52 C5
Mons Belgium 67 B6
Montague Seamount *Undersea feature* Atlantic Ocean 43 H1
Montana *State* USA 22 C2
Montauban France 71 B6
Mont Blanc *Peak* France/Italy 60 D4
Mont-de-Marsan France 70 B6
Monte-Carlo Monaco 71 E6
Montecristi Dominican Republic 35 E3
Montego Bay Jamaica 34 C3
Montenegro *Republic* Yugoslavia 81 D5
Monterey California, USA 25 B6
Montería Colombia 38 B2
Montero Bolivia 40 D4
Monterrey Mexico 31 E2
Montes Claros Brazil 41 G4
Montevideo *Capital of* Uruguay 42 C5
Montgomery Alabama, USA 28 D3
Montpelier Vermont, USA 21 F2
Montpellier France 71 C6

Montréal Canada 19 E4

Montreux Switzerland 75 A5

Montserrat *External territory* UK, West Indies 35

Monument Valley *Valley* SW USA 26 C1

Monywa Myanmar 118 A3

Monza Italy 76 B2

Moora Australia 129 B6

Moorhead Minnesota, USA 23 E2

Moosonee Canada 18 C3

Mopti Mali 53 E3

Morava *River* C Europe 79 B6 80 E4

Moravská Ostrava *see* Ostrava

Morawhanna Guyana 39 F2

Moray Firth *Inlet* Scotland, UK 68 C3

Moree Australia 130 C2

Morehead City North Carolina, USA 29 G2

Morelia Mexico 31 E4

Morena, Sierra *Mountain range* Spain 72 D4

Morghâb *River* Afghanistan/Turkmenistan 102 D4

Morioka Japan 110 D3

Morocco *Country* N Africa 50

Morogoro Tanzania 55 C7

Morondava Madagascar 59 F2

Moroni *Capital of* Comoros 59 F2

Morotai, Pulau *Island* Indonesia 121 F3

Moscow *Capital of* Russian Federation *Rus.* Moskva 90 B4 94 B2

Mosel *River* W Europe *Fr.* Moselle 75 A5

Moselle *River* W Europe *Ger.* Mosel 67 E8 70 E4

Moshi Tanzania 55 C7

Moskva *see* Moscow

Mosquito Coast *Coastal region* Nicaragua 33 E3

Moss Norway 65 B6

Mossendjo Congo 57 B6

Mossoró Brazil 41 H2

Most Czech Republic *Ger.* Brüx 78 A4

Mostaganem Algeria 50 D1

Mostar Bosnia & Herzegovina 80 C4

Mosul *see* Al Mawşil

Motril Spain 73 E5

Moulins France 70 C4

Moulmein Myanmar 118 B4

Moundou Chad 56 C4

Mount Gambier Australia 130 A4

Mount Isa Australia 126 A5 130 A1

Mount Vernon Illinois, USA 20 B5

Mouscron Belgium 67 A6

Moyale Kenya 55 C5

Moyobamba Peru 40 B2

Mozambique *Country* SE Africa 59

Mozambique Channel *Sea Feature* Indian Ocean 59 H3

Mozambique Ridge *Undersea feature* Indian Ocean 49 D8

Mozyr' *see* Mazyr

Mpika Zambia 59 E2

Mtwara Tanzania 55 C8

Muang Khammouan Laos 118 D4

Muang Không Laos 119 D5

Muang Xaignabouri Laos 118 C3

Mufulira Zambia 58 D2

Mugla Turkey 96 A4

Mukacheve Ukraine 88 B2

Mulhacén Peak Spain 60 C5

Mulhouse France 70 E4

Mull *Island* Scotland, UK 68 B3

Muller, Pegunungan *Mountains* Indonesia 120 D4

Multán Pakistan 114 C2

Mumbai *see* Bombay

Muna, Pulau *Island* Indonesia 121 E4

München Germany *Eng.* Munich 75 C6

Muncie Indiana, USA 20 C4

Munich *see* München

Münster Germany 74 A4

Muonio *River* Finland/Sweden 64 D3

Muqdisho *see* Mogadishu

Mur *River* C Europe 75 D7

Murcia *Region* Spain 73 F4

Mures *River* Hungary/Romania 79 D7

Murfreesboro Tennessee, USA 28 D1

Murgab Tajikistan 103 F3

Murgab *River* Turkmenistan *var.* Murghab 102 D3

Murghab *see* Murgab

Müritz *Lake* Germany 74 D3

Murmansk Russian Federation 90 C2 94 C1

Murray *River* Australia 130 A3

Murrumbidgee *River* Australia 130 B3

Murska Sobota Slovenia 80 B2

Murzuq Libya 51 F3

Muş Turkey 97 F3

Muscat *Capital of* Oman *Ar.* Masqaţ 101 E5

Musgrave Ranges *Mountain range* Australia 129 D5

Mwanza Tanzania 55 B6

Mwene-Ditu Zaire 57 D7

Mweru, Lake *Lake* Zaire/Zambia 57 D7

Myanmar *Country* SE Asia *var.* Burma 118-119

Mykolayiv Ukraine *Rus.* Nikolayev 89 E4

Mysore India 116 D2

Mzuzu Malawi 59 E2

N

Naberezhnyye Chelny Russian Federation *prev.* Brezhnev 91 C5

Nacala Mozambique 59 F2

Næstved Denmark 65 D8

Naga Philippines 120 E1

Nagano Japan 110 C4

Nagasaki Japan 111 A6

Nägercoil India 116 D3

Nagorno-Karabakh *Region* Azerbaijan 97 G2

Nagoya Japan 111 C5

Nägpur India 114 D4

Nagqu China 106 C5

Nagykanizsa Hungary *Ger.* Grosskanizsa 79 C7

Nagyszombat *see* Trnava

Naha Japan 111 A8

Nain Canada 19 N2

Nairobi *Capital of* Kenya 55 C6

Najaf *see* An Najaf

Najrān Saudi Arabia 101 B6

Nakamura Japan 111 B6

Nakhichevan' *see* Naxçıvan

Nakhodka Russian Federation 94 C3

Nakhon Ratchasima Thailand 119 C5

Nakhon Sawan Thailand 119 C5

Nakhon Si Thammarat Thailand 119 C6

Nakina Canada 18 B3

Nakskov Denmark 65 D8

Nakuru Kenya 55 C6

Nal'chik Russian Federation 91 A7 94 A4

Namangan Uzbekistan 103 E2

Nam Đinh Vietnam 119 E5

Namib Desert *Desert* Namibia 58 B3

Namibe Angola 58 B2

Namibia *Country* southern Africa 58

Nampa Idaho, USA 24 D3

Namp'o North Korea 108 E4

Nampula Mozambique 59 F2

Namur Belgium 67 C6

Nanchang China 109 C6

Nancy France 70 D3

Nāndēd India 114 D5 116 D1

Nanjing China 109 D5

Nanning China 109 B7

Nanortalik Greenland 62 C4

Nantes France 70 B4

Napier New Zealand 131 H2

Naples *see* Napoli

Napo *River* Ecuador/Peru 40 B2

Napoli Italy *Eng.* Naples 77 D5

Narbonne France 71 C6

Nares Plain *Undersea feature* Atlantic Ocean 15 F4

Nares Strait *Sea feature* Canada/Greenland 62 A2

Narew *River* Poland 78 E3

Narmada *River* India 114 D4

Narsaq Greenland 62 C4

Narsaq Kujalleq Greenland 62 C4

Narva Estonia 86 E2

Narva *River* Estonia/Russian Federation 86 E2

Narva Bay *Sea feature* Gulf of Finland *Est.* Narva Laht, *Rus.* Narvskiy Zaliv 86 E2

Narva Laht *see* Narva Bay

Narvik Norway 64 C3

Narvskiy Zaliv *see* Narva Bay

Naryn Kyrgyzstan 103 G2

Naryn *River* Kyrgyzstan/Uzbekistan 103 F2

Nāshik India 114 C5

Nashville Tennessee, USA 28 D1

Nâsir, Buheiret *Reservoir* Egypt 55 B2

Nasiriya *see* An Nāşirīyah

Nassau *Capital of* Bahamas 34 C1

Natal Brazil 41 H3

Natitingou Benin 53 F4

Natuna, Kepulauan *Island group* Indonesia 120 C3

Nauru *Country* Pacific Ocean 126 D3

Navapolatsk Belarus *Rus.* Novopolotsk 87 D5

Navassa Island *External territory* USA, West Indies 34 D3

Navoi Uzbekistan *Uzb.* Nawoly 102 D2

Nawābshāh Pakistan 114 B3

Nawoly *see* Navoi

Naxçıvan Azerbaijan *Rus.* Nakhichevan' 97 G3

Náxos *Island* Greece 85 D6

Nazareth *see* Nazerat

Nazca Peru 40 B4

Naẕerat Israel *Eng.* Nazareth 99 A5

Nazrēt Ethiopia 55 C5

Nazwá Oman 101 E5

N'Dalatando Angola 58 B1

Ndélé Central African Republic 56 C4

N'Djamena *Capital of* Chad 56 B3

Ndola Zambia 58 D2

Nebitdag Turkmenistan 102 B2

Nebraska *State* USA 22-23 E3

Neches *River* S USA 27 H3

Neckar *River* Germany 75 B6

Necochea Argentina 45 D5

Neftezavodsk *see* Seydi

Negēlē Ethiopia 55 C5

Negev *see* HaNegev

Negro, Río *River* Argentina 45 C5

Negro, Rio *River* Brazil/Uruguay 40 D2

Negro, Rio *River* N South America 38 D3

Negros *Island* Philippines 121 E2

Neiva Colombia 38 B3

Nellore India 117 E2

Nelson New Zealand 131 G3

Neman *River* NE Europe *Bel.* Nyoman, *Lith.* Nemunas, *Ger.* Memel, *Pol.* Niemen 86 B4

Nemunas *see* Neman

Nemuro Japan 110 E2

Nepal *Country* S Asia 115

Nepalganj Nepal 115 E3

Neretva *River* Bosnia & Herzegovina 80 C4

Neris *River* Belarus/Lithuania *Bel.* Viliya, *Pol.* Wilja 86 C4

Ness, Loch *Lake* Scotland, UK 68 C3

Netherlands *Country* W Europe *var.* Holland 66-67

Netherlands Antilles *External territory* Netherlands, West Indies *prev.* Dutch West Indies 36 C1

Netze *see* Noteć

Neubrandenburg Germany 74 D3

Neuchâtel, Lac de *Lake* Switzerland 75 A7

Neuhäusl *see* Nové Zámky

Neumünster Germany 74 B2

Neuquén Argentina 45 C5

Neusiedler See *Lake* Austria/Hungary 75 E7

Neusohl *see* Banská Bystrica

Neutra *see* Nitra

Nevada *State* USA 24-25

Nevel' Russian Federation 90 A4

Nevers France 70 C4

Nevşehir Turkey 96 D3

Nevşehir Turkey 96 D3

New Amsterdam Guyana 39 G2

Newark New Jersey, USA 21 F3

New Britain *Island* Papua New Guinea 126 C3

Oka *River* Russian Federation 95 E4

Okahandja Namibia 58 C3

Okavango *River var.* Cubango southern Africa 58 C2

Okavango Delta *Wetland* Botswana 58 C3

Okayama Japan 111 B5

Okazaki Japan 111 C5

Okeechobee, Lake *Lake* Florida, USA 29 F4

Okhotsk Russian Federation 95 G3

Okhotsk, Sea of Pacific Ocean 122 C1

Okinawa *Island* Japan 111 A8

Oki-shotō *Island group* Japan 111 B5

Oklahoma *State* USA 27 F1

Oklahoma City Oklahoma, USA 27 F2

Okushiri-tō *Island* Japan 110 C2

Okāra Pakistan 114 C2

Öland *Island* Sweden 65 C7

Olavarría Argentina 44 D4

Olbia Italy 77 A5

Oldenburg Germany 74 B3

Oleksandriya Ukraine *Rus.* Aleksandriya 89 E3

Olenëk Russian Federation 95 E3

Olhão Portugal 72 C5

Olita *see* Alytus

Olmaliq *see* Almalyk

Olmütz *see* Olomouc

Olomouc Czech Republic *Ger.* Olmütz 79 C5

Olsztyn Poland *Ger.* Allenstein 78 D2

Olt *River* Romania 88 B5

Olten Switzerland 75 B7

Olympia Washington, USA 24 B2

Omaha Nebraska, USA 23 F4

Oman *Country* SW Asia 101 D6

Oman, Gulf of *Sea feature* Indian Ocean 112 B2

Omdurman Sudan 54 B4

Omsk Russian Federation 94 C4

Ondangwa Namibia 58 C3

Onega *River* Russian Federation 90 B4

Onega, Lake *see* Onezhskoye Ozero

Onezhskoye Ozero *Lake* Russian Federation *Eng.* Lake Onega 90 B3

Ongole India 117 E2

Onitsha Nigeria 53 G5

Ontario *Province* Canada 18 B3

Ontario, Lake *Lake* Canada/USA 15 F3

Oostende Belgium *Eng.* Ostend 67 A5

Oosterschelde *Inlet* Netherlands 66 B4

Opole Poland *Ger.* Oppeln 78 C4

Oporto *see* Porto

Oppeln *see* Opole

Oradea Romania 88 B3

Oran Algeria 50 D1

Orange Australia 130 C3

Orange River *River* southern Africa 58 C4

Oranjestad Netherlands Antilles 35 E5

Ord *River* Australia 128 D3

Ordu Turkey 96 D2

Ordzhonikidze *see* Vladikavkaz

Örebro Sweden 65 C6

Oregon *State* USA 24

Orël Russian Federation 81 A5

Orem Utah, USA 22 B4

Orenburg Russian Federation 91 C6 94 B4

Orense *see* Ourense

Orestiáda Greece 84 D3

Orhon *River* Mongolia 107 E2

Orinoco *River* Colombia/Venezuela 39 E3

Orissa *State* India 115 E5

Oristano Italy 77 A5

Orizaba, Pico de *see* Citlaltépetl

Orkney *Islands* Scotland, UK 68 C2

Orlando Florida, USA 29 E4

Orléans France 70 C4

Ormsö *see* Vormsi

Örnsköldsvik Sweden 65 C5

Orontes *River* SW Asia 98 B3

Orosirá Rodópis *see* Rhodope Mountains

Orsha Belarus 87 E5

Orsk Russian Federation 91 D6 94 B4

Oruro Bolivia 40 C4

Ōsaka Japan 111 C5

Ösel *see* Saaremaa

Osh Kyrgyzstan 103 F2

Oshawa Canada 18 D5

Oshkosh Wisconsin, USA 20 B2

Osijek Croatia 80 C3

Oslo *Capital of* Norway 65 B6

Osmaniye Turkey 96 D4

Osnabrück Germany 74 B4

Osorno Chile 45 B5

Oss Netherlands 66 D4

Ossora Russian Federation 95 H2

Ostend *see* Oostende

Östersund Sweden 65 C5

Ostfriesische Inseln *Islands* Germany *Eng.* East Frisian Islands 74 A3

Ostrava Czech Republic *Ger.* Mährisch-Ostrau, *prev.* Moravská Ostrava 79 C5

Ostrołęka Poland 78 D3

Ostrowiec Świętokrzyski Poland 78 D4

Ōsumi-shotō *Island group* Japan 111 A7

Otaru Japan 110 D2

Otra *River* Norway 65 A6

Otranto Italy 77 E5

Otranto, Strait of *Sea feature* Albania/Italy 81 C6

Ottawa *Capital of* Canada 18 D5

Ottawa *River* Canada 18 D4

Ou *River* Laos 118 C3

Ouachita *River* SE USA 28 B2

Ouagadougou *Capital of* Burkina 53 E4

Ouahigouya Burkina 53 E3

Ouargla Algeria 51 E2

Oudtshoorn South Africa 58 C5

Ouémé *River* Benin 53 F4

Ouessant, Île d' *Island* France 70 A3

Ouésso Congo 57 C5

Oujda Morocco 50 D2

Oulu Finland 64 D4

Oulu *River* Finland 64 D4

Oulujärvi *Lake* Finland 64 E4

Ounas *River* Finland 64 D3

Pechora *River* Russian Federation 90 D3

Pecos Texas, USA 27 E3

Pecos *River* SW USA 26 D2

Pécs Hungary *Ger.* Fünfkirchen 79 C7

Pegu Myanmar 118 B4

Peipsi Järv *see* Peipus, Lake

Peipus, Lake *Lake* Estonia/Russian Federation *Est.* Peipsi Järv, *Rus.* Chudskoye Ozero 86 D2

Peiraías Greece *var.* Piraiévs, *Eng.* Piraeus 83 F3 85 C5

Peking *see* Beijing

Pelagie, Isola *Island* Italy 77 B8

Peloponnese *see* Pelopónnisos

Pelopónnisos *Peninsula* Greece *Eng.* Peloponnese 85 B6

Pelotas Brazil 42 C4

Pelotas *River* Brazil 42 D3

Pematangsiantar Indonesia 120 A3

Pemba *Island* Tanzania 49 E5

Pendleton Oregon, USA 24 C2

Pennines *Hills* England, UK 68 D4

Pennsylvania *State* USA 20-21

Penong Australia 129 D6

Penonomé Panama 33 F5

Pensacola Florida, USA 28 D3

Penza Russian Federation 91 B5

Penzance England, UK 69 C7

Peoria Illinois, USA 20 B4

Pereira Colombia 38 B3

Périgueux France 71 B5

Perm' Russian Federation *prev.* Molotov 91 D5 94 B3

Pernau *see* Pärnu

Pernik Bulgaria *prev.* Dimitrovo 84 B2

Pernov *see* Pärnu

Perpignan France 71 C6

Persian Gulf *Sea feature* Arabian Sea *var.* The Gulf 112 B2

Perth Australia 129 B6

Perth Scotland, UK 68 C3

Perth Basin *Undersea feature* Indian Ocean 124 A3

Peru *C South America* 40

Peru Basin *Undersea feature* Pacific Ocean 123 G4

Peru-Chile Trench *Undersea feature* Pacific Ocean 123 G4

Perugia Italy 76 C4

Pescara Italy 76 D4

Peshāwar Pakistan 114 C1

Petaḥ Tiqwa Israel 99 A5

Peterborough England, UK 69 E6

Peterborough Canada 18 D5

Peter the First Island *Island* Antarctica 132 A4

Petra Jordan 99 B6

Petrich Bulgaria 84 B3

Petroaleksandrovsk *see* Turtkul'

Petrograd *see* St Petersburg

Petropavlovsk Russian Federation 94 C4

Petropavlovsk-Kamchatskiy Russian Federation 95 H3

Petrozavodsk Russian Federation 90 B3

Pevek Russian Federation 95 G1

Pforzheim Germany 75 B6

Phangan, Ko *Island* Thailand 119 C6

Philadelphia Pennsylvania, USA 21 F4

Philippines *Country* Asia 121

Philippine Sea *Pacific Ocean* 121 F1

Philippopolis *see* Plovdiv

Phnom Penh *Capital of* Cambodia 119 D6

Phoenix Arizona, USA 26 B2

Phoenix Islands *Island group* Kiribati 127 F3

Phôngsali Laos 118 C3

Phuket Thailand 119 B7

Phuket, Ko *Island* Thailand 119 B7

Phumĭ Sâmraông Cambodia 119 D5

Piacenza Italy 76 B2

Pianosa *Island* Italy 76 D4

Piatra-Neamţ Romania 88 C3

Piave *River* Italy 76 D2

Pielinen *Lake* Finland 64 E4

Pierre South Dakota, USA 23 E3

Piešťany Slovakia *Ger.* Pistyan, *Hung.* Pöstyén 79 C6

Pietermaritzburg South Africa 58 D4

Pihkva Järv *see* Pskov, Lake

Piła Poland *Ger.* Schneidemühl 78 C3

Pilar Paraguay 42 B3

Pilchilemu Chile 44 B4

Pilcomayo *River* C South America 42 B3 44 D2

Pillau *see* Baltiysk

Pilsen *see* Plzeň

Pinang, Pulau *Island* Malaysia 120 B3

Pinar del Río Cuba 34 A2

Píndos *Mountain range* Greece *Eng.* Pindus Mountains 61 E5 84 A4

Pindus Mountains *see* Píndos

Pine Bluff Arkansas, USA 28 B2

Pinega *River* Russian Federation 90 C3

Pineiós *River* Greece 84 B4

Pine Island Bay *Sea feature* Antarctica 132 B3

Ping, Mae Nam *River* Thailand 118 C4

Pingxiang China 109 B7

Pínnes, Ákra *Coastal feature* Greece 84 C4

Pinsk Belarus *Pol.* Pińsk 87 B4

Piraeus *see* Peiraías

Piraiévs *see* Peiraías

Pisa Italy 76 B3

Pisco Peru 40 B4

Pishpek *see* Bishkek

Pistyan *see* Piešťany

Pitcairn Islands *External territory* UK, Pacific Ocean 123 E4

Piteå Sweden 64 D4

Piteşti Romania 88 C4

Pittsburgh Pennsylvania, USA 21 E4

Pituffik Greenland 62 A2

Piura Peru 40 A2

Pivdennyy Bug *River* Ukraine 89 E3

Plasencia Spain 72 D3

Plate *River* Argentina/Uruguay 42 B5 44 B4

Platte *River* C USA 23 E4

Plattensee *see* Balaton

Plenty, Bay of *Sea feature* New Zealand 131 H2

Pleven Bulgaria 84 C1

Płock Poland 78 D3

Prome Myanmar 118 A4

Prossnitz *see* Prostějov

Prostějov Czech Republic
Ger. Prossnitz 79 C5

Provence *Region* France 71 D6

Providence Rhode Island, USA
21 G3

Providencia, Isla de *Island*
Colombia 33 E3 34 B4

Provo Utah, USA 22 B4

Prudhoe Bay Alaska, USA
16 D2

Prydz Bay *Sea feature* Antarctica
133 G2

Przheval'sk *see* Karakol

Pskov Russian Federation 90 A4

Pskov, Lake *Lake*
Estonia/Russian Federation
Est. Pihkva Järv,
Rus. Pskovskoye Ozero 86 D3

Pskovskoye Ozero *see* Pskov,
Lake

Ptich' *see* Ptsich

Ptsich *River* Belarus
Rus. Ptich' 87 D6

Pucallpa Peru 40 B3

Puebla Mexico 31 F4

Puerto Aisén Chile 45 B6

Puerto Bahía Negra Paraguay
42 B1

Puerto Barrios Guatemala 32 C2

Puerto Busch Bolivia 40 D5

Puerto Carreño Colombia 38 D2

Puerto Cortés Honduras 32 C2

Puerto Deseado Argentina
45 C7

Puerto Maldonado Peru 40 C4

Puerto Montt Chile 45 B5

Puerto Natales Chile 45 B7

Puerto Plata Dominican
Republic 35 E3

Puerto Princesa Philippines
120 E2

Puerto Rico *External territory*
USA, West Indies 35 F3

Puerto Rico Trench *Undersea
feature* Caribbean Sea 35 F3

Puerto Santa Cruz Argentina
45 C7

Puerto Suárez Bolivia 40 D5

Puerto Vallarta Mexico 30 D4

Puerto Williams Chile 45 C8

Pula Croatia 80 B2

Punakha Bhutan 115 G3

Punata Bolivia 40 C4

Pune India *prev.* Poona 114 C5
116 C1

Punjab *State* India 114 C2

Puno Peru 40 C4

Punta Arenas Chile
prev. Magallanes 45 B8

Puntarenas Costa Rica 32 D4

Purmerend Netherlands 66 C3

Purus *River* Brazil/Peru 40 C3

Pusan South Korea 108 E4

Putumayo *River* NW South
America 38 C4

Pyandzh *see* Panj

Pyapon Myanmar 118 B4

Pyarnu *see* Pärnu

Pyinmana Myanmar 118 B3

Pyongyang *Capital of* North
Korea 108 E4

Pyramiden Svalbard 63 G2

Pyramid Lake *Lake* Nevada,
USA 25 C5

Pyrenees *Mountain range* SW
Europe 60 C5

Q

Qaanaaq Greenland *var.* Thule
62 A2

Qal'eh-ye Now Afghanistan
102 D4

Qamdo China 106 D5

Qandahār *see* Kandahār

Qaqortoq Greenland 62 C4

Qara Qum *see* Karakumy

Qarshi *see* Karshi

Qasigiannguit Greenland 62 B3

Qatar *Country* SW Asia 101 D5

Qattara Depression *see* Qattâra,
Monkhafad el

Qattâra, Monkhafad el *Desert
basin* Egypt *Eng.* Qattara
Depression 48 C2 54 A1

Qena Egypt 54 B2

Qeqertarsuaq Greenland 62 B3

Qeqertarsuaq *Island* Greenland
62 B3

Qeqertarsuatsiaat Greenland
62 B3

Qilian Shan *Mountain range*
China 106 D4

Qingdao China 108 D4

Qinghai Hu *Lake* China *var.*
Koko Nor 106 D4

Qing-Zang Gaoyuan *Plateau*
China *Eng.* Plateau of Tibet
104 C2 106 B4

Qin Ling *Mountains* China
109 B5

Qiqihar China 108 D3

Qizilqum *see* Kyzyl Kum

Qom Iran *var.* Kum 100 C3

Qondūz *River* Afghanistan
103 E4

Qondūz *see* Kunduz

Quba Azerbaijan *Rus.* Kuba
97 H2

Québec Canada 19 E4

Québec *Province* Canada 18 D3

Queen Charlotte Islands *Islands*
Canada 16 D5

Queen Charlotte Sound *Sea
feature* Canada 16 D5

Queen Elizabeth Islands *Islands*
Canada 17 F1

Queen Maud Land *Region*
Antarctica 133 E1

Queensland *State* Australia 126
B5 130 B1

Queenstown New Zealand
131 F1

Quelimane Mozambique 59 E3

Querétaro Mexico 31 E4

Quetta Pakistan 112 B2

Quezaltenango Guatemala
32 B2

Quibdó Colombia 38 B2

Quimper France 70 A3

Qui Nhon Vietnam 119 E5

Quito *Capital of* Ecuador 38 A4

Qüqon *see* Kokand

Qyteti Stalin *see* Kuçovë

R

Raab *see* Győr

Raab *see* Rába

Rába *River* Austria/Hungary
Ger. Raab 79 C7

Rabat *Capital of* Morocco 50 C2

Race, Cape *Coastal feature*
Canada 15 G3 19 H4

Rach Gia Vietnam 119 D6

Sakarya *see* Adapazarı

Sakhalin *Island* Russian Federation 95 H4

Salado *River* Argentina 44 C3

Şalālah Oman 101 D6

Salamanca Spain 72 D2

Sala y Gómez *Island* Chile, Pacific Ocean 123 F4

Saldus Latvia *Ger.* Frauenburg 86 B3

Sale Australia 130 B4

Salekhard Russian Federation 94 D3

Salem India 116 D2

Salem Oregon, USA 24 B3

Salerno Italy 77 D5

Salerno, Golfo di *Sea feature* Italy 77 D5

Salihorsk Belarus *Rus.* Soligorsk 87 C6

Salima Malawi 59 E2

Salina *Island* Italy 77 D6

Salina Utah, USA 22 B4

Salinas California, USA 25 B6

Salinas Grandes *Lowpoint* Argentina 44 C3

Salisbury England, UK 69 D7

Salisbury Island *Island* Canada 18 D1

Salonica *see* Thessaloníki

Salso *River* Italy 77 C7

Salt *see* As Salṭ

Salta Argentina 44 C2

Saltillo Mexico 31 E2

Salt Lake City Utah, USA 22 B2

Salto Uruguay 42 B4

Salton Sea *Lake* California, USA 25 D8

Salvador Brazil 41 H4

Salween *River* SE Asia 104 C3

Salzburg Austria 75 D7

Salzgitter Germany 74 C4

Samaná Dominican Republic 35 E3

Samar *Island* Philippines 121 F2

Samara Russian Federation 91 C6 94 B3

Samarinda Indonesia 120 D4

Samarkand Uzbekistan 102 D3

Sambre *River* Belgium 67 B7

Samobor Croatia 80 B2

Sámos *Island* Greece 85 D5

Samothrace *see* Samothráki

Samothráki *Island* Greece *Eng.* Samothrace 84 D3

Samsun Turkey 96 D2

Samui, Ko *Island group* Thailand 119 C6

San *River* Cambodia/Vietnam 118-119

San *River* Poland 79 E5

Saña Peru 40 A3

Sana *Capital of* Yemen *var.* Şan'â' 101 B7

San Ambrosio, Isla *Island* 44 A3

San Andrés, Isla de *Island* Colombia 33 E3 34 B5

San Angelo Texas, USA 27 F3

San Antonio Chile 44 B4

San Antonio Texas, USA 27 F4

San Antonio *River* S USA 27 G4

San Antonio Oeste Argentina 45 C5

Sanāw Yemen 101 C6

San Bernardino California, USA 25 C7

San Carlos Uruguay 42 C5

San Carlos de Bariloche Argentina 45 B5

San Clemente Island *Island* W USA 25 C8

San Cristóbal Venezuela 38 C2

San Diego California, USA 25 C8

San Félix, Isla *Island* Chile 44 A2

San Fernando Chile 44 B4

San Fernando Trinidad & Tobago 35 G5

San Fernando Venezuela 38 D2

San Francisco California, USA 25 B6

San Ignacio Belize 32 C1

San Ignacio Paraguay 42 B3

San Joaquin *River* W USA 25 B6

San Jorge, Golfo *Sea feature* Argentina 37 C6

San José *Capital of* Costa Rica 32 D4

San José California, USA 25 B6

San José del Guaviare Colombia 38 C3

San Juan Argentina 44 B3

San Juan *River* Costa Rica/Nicaragua 32 D4

San Juan *Capital of* Puerto Rico 35 F3

San Juan de los Morros Venezuela 38 D1

Sankt Gallen Switzerland 75 B7

Sankt Martin *see* Martin

Sankt-Peterburg *see* St Petersburg

Sankt Pölten Austria 75 E6

Şanlıurfa Turkey *prev.* Urfa 96 E4

San Lorenzo Honduras 32 C3

San Luis Potosí Mexico 31 E3

San Marino *Country* S Europe 76 C3

San Matías, Golfo *Sea feature* Argentina 37 C6

San Miguel El Salvador 32 C3

San Miguel de Tucumán Argentina 44 C3

San Nicolas Island *Island* W USA 25 C8

San Pedro Sula Honduras 32 C2

San Remo Italy 76 A3

San Salvador *Capital of* El Salvador 32 C3

San Salvador de Jujuy Argentina 44 C2

San Sebastián Spain *Bas.* Donostia 73 E1

Santa Ana El Salvador 32 B2

Santa Ana California, USA 25 C8

Santa Barbara California, USA 25 B7

Santa Catalina Island *Island* W USA 25 C8

Santa Clara Cuba 34 B2

Santa Cruz Bolivia 40 D4

Santa Cruz California, USA 25 B6

Santa Cruz Islands *Island group* Solomon Islands 126 C3

Santa Fe Argentina 44 D3

Santa Fe New Mexico, USA 26 D2

Santa Maria Brazil 42 C4

Santa Marta Colombia 38 C1

Santander Spain 73 E1

Santanilla, Islas *Islands* Honduras 33 E1

Santarém Brazil 41 E2

Santarém Portugal 72 C3

Santa Rosa Argentina 45 C4

Santa Rosa California, USA 25 A6

Santa Rosa de Copán Honduras 32 C2

Santa Rosa Island *Island* W USA 25 B8

Santee *River* SE USA 29 F2

Santiago *Capital of* Chile 44 B4

Santiago Dominican Republic 35 E3

Santiago Panama 33 F5

Santiago Spain 72 C1

Santiago de Cuba Cuba 34 C3

Santiago del Estero Argentina 44 C3

Santo Domingo *Capital of* Dominican Republic 35 E3

Santo Domingo de los Colorados Ecuador 38 A4

Santos Brazil 43 E2

Santos Plateau *Undersea feature* Atlantic Ocean 43 E3

Sanya China 109 B8

São Borja Brazil 42 C3

São Francisco *River* Brazil 41 G3

São José do Rio Preto Brazil 42 D1

São Luís Brazil 41 G2

Saône *River* France 70 D4

São Paulo Brazil 41 F5 43 E2

São Roque, Cabo de *Coastal feature* Brazil 36 E3

São Tomé *Capital of* Sao Tome & Principe 57 A5

São Tomé *Island* Sao Tome & Principe 57 A6

Sao Tome & Principe *Country* W Africa 57

São Vicente, Cabo de *Coastal feature* Portugal *Eng.* Cape St Vincent 60 B5 72 B5

Sapporo Japan 110 D2

Saragossa *see* Zaragoza

Sarajevo *Capital of* Bosnia & Herzegovina 80 C4

Sarandë Albania 81 D7

Saransk Russian Federation 91 B5

Saratov Russian Federation 91 B6

Sarawak *State* Malaysia 120 D3

Sardegna *Island* Italy *Eng.* Sardinia 77 B5 83 D3

Sardinia *see* Sardegna

Sarema *see* Saaremaa

Sargasso Sea Atlantic Ocean 46 B4

Sargodha Pakistan 114 C2

Sarh Chad 56 C4

Saruhan *see* Manisa

Sasebo Japan 111 A6

Saskatchewan *Province* Canada 17 F5

Saskatchewan *River* Canada 17 F5

Saskatoon Canada 17 F5

Sassari Italy 77 A5

Satu Mare Romania 88 B3

Saudi Arabia *Country* SW Asia 100-101

Sault Sainte Marie Canada 18 C4

Sault Sainte Marie Michigan, USA 20 C1

Saurimo Angola 58 C1

Sava *River* SE Europe 80 C3

Savannah Georgia, USA 29 F3

Savannah *River* SE USA 29 F2

Savannakhét Laos 118 D4

Savissivik Greenland 62 A2

Savona Italy 76 A3

Savonlinna Finland 65 E5

Şawqirah Oman 101 D6

Sayat Turkmenistan 102 D3

Sayhūt Yemen 101 D7

Saynshand Mongolia 107 E2

Say 'ün Yemen 101 C6

Schaffhausen Switzerland 75 B7

Schaulen *see* Šiauliai

Schefferville Canada 19 E2

Scheldt *River* W Europe 67 B5

Schiermonnikoog *Island* Netherlands 66 D1

Schneidemühl *see* Piła

Schwäbische Alb *Mountains* Germany 75 B6

Schwarzwald *Forested mountain region* Germany *Eng.* Black Forest 75 B6

Schwerin Germany 74 C3

Schweriner See *Lake* Germany 74 C3

Scilly, Isles of *Islands* UK 69 B8

Scotia Ridge *Undersea feature* Atlantic Ocean 47 B7

Scotia Sea Atlantic Ocean 47 B7

Scotland *National region* UK 68

Scottsbluff Nebraska, USA 22 D3

Scottsdale Arizona, USA 26 B2

Scranton Pennsylvania, USA 21 F3

Scutari, Lake *Lake* Albania/Yugoslavia 81 C5

Seattle Washington, USA 24 B2

Ségou Mali 52 D3

Segovia Spain 73 E2

Segura *River* Spain 73 E4

Seikan Tunnel *Tunnel* Japan 110 D3

Seinäjoki Finland 65 D5

Seine *River* France 70 C3

Sekondi-Takoradi Ghana 53 E5

Selfoss Iceland 63 E4

Selma Alabama, USA 28 D3

Semara Western Sahara 50 B3

Semarang Indonesia 120 C5

Semipalatinsk Kazakhstan 94 D4

Sên *River* Cambodia 118-119 D5

Sendai Japan 110 D4

Senegal *Country* W Africa 52

Senegal *River* Africa 52 B3

Seoul *Capital of* South Korea *Kor.* Sŏul 108 E4

Sept-Iles Canada 19 F3

Seraing Belgium 67 D6

Seram *Island* Indonesia 121 F4

Serbia *Republic* Yugoslavia 80 D3

Seremban Malaysia 120 B3

Sermersuaq *Region* Greenland 62 B2

Serov Russian Federation 94 C3

Serpent's Mouth, The *Sea feature* Trinidad & Tobago/Venezuela *Sp.* Boca de la Serpiente 39 F1

Serra do Mar *Mountains* Brazil 42 D3

Sérres Greece 84 C3

Sétif Algeria 51 E1

Setúbal Portugal 72 C4

Seul, Lake *Lake* Canada 18 A3

Sevana Lich *Lake* Armenia 97 G2

Sevastopol' Ukraine 89 C5

Springfield Illinois, USA 20 B4

Springfield Massachusetts, USA 21 G3

Springfield Missouri, USA 23 F5

Springfield Oregon, USA 24 B3

Srebrenica Bosnia & Herzegovina 80 C4

Sri Lanka *Country* S Asia *prev.* Ceylon 117

Srinagar India 114 D1

Srinagarind Reservoir *Reservoir* Thailand 119 C5

Stalinabad *see* Dushanbe

Stalingrad *see* Volgograd

Stalin Peak *see* Communism Peak

Stalinsk *see* Novokuznetsk

Stambul *see* İstanbul

Stanleyville *see* Kisangani

Stanovoy Range *Mountain range* Russian Federation 93 F3

Stara Planina *see* Balkan Mountains

Stara Zagora Bulgaria 84 D2

Stavanger Norway 65 A6

Stavropol' Russian Federation 91 A7 94 A3

Steinamanger *see* Szombathely

Steinkjer Norway 64 B4

Stepanakert *see* Xankändi

Stettin *see* Szczecin

Stewart Island *Island* New Zealand 131 F5

Ştip Macedonia 81 E5

Stirling Scotland, UK 68 C4

Stockerau Austria 75 E6

Stockholm *Capital of* Sweden 65 C6

Stockton California, USA 25 B6

Stœng Treng Cambodia 119 D5

Stoke-on-Trent England, UK 69 D6

Stolp *see* Słupsk

Stornoway Scotland, UK 68 B2

Stralsund Germany 74 D2

Stranraer Scotland, UK 68 C4

Strasbourg France *Ger.* Strassburg 70 E4

Stratford-upon-Avon England, UK 69 D6

Stratonice Czech Republic 79 A5

Strimon *see* Struma

Stromboli *Island* Italy 77 D6

Struma *prev.* Ceylon Bulgaria / Greece *Gk.* Strimon, *var.* Strymon 84 C3

Strumica Macedonia 81 E5

Strymon *see* Struma

Stuhlweissenburg *see* Székesfehérvár

Stuttgart Germany 75 B6

Subotica Yugoslavia 80 D2

Suceava Romania 88 C3

Sucre *Capital of* Bolivia 40 C5

Sudan *Country* NE Africa 54-55

Sudbury Canada 18 C4

Sudd *Region* Sudan 55 B5

Sudeten *Mountains* Central Europe *var.* Sudetes, Sudetic Mountains, *Cz. / Pol.* Sudety 79 B5

Sudetes *see* Sudeten

Sudetic Mountains *see* Sudeten

Sudety *see* Sudeten

Suez Egypt 54 B1

Suez, Gulf of *Sea feature* Red Sea 99 A8

Suez Canal *Canal* Egypt *Ar.* Qanāt as Suways 48 D2

Şuḩār Oman 101 D5

Sühbaatar Mongolia 107 E1

Sukhumi *see* Sokhumi

Sukkur Pakistan 114 B3

Sula, Kepulauan *Island group* Indonesia 121 F4

Sulawesi *Island* Indonesia *Eng.* Celebes 121 E4

Sulu Archipelago *Island group* Philippines 121 E3

Sülüktü *see* Sulyukta

Sulu Sea Pacific Ocean 121 E2

Sulyukta Kyrgyzstan *Kir.* Sülüktü 103 E2

Sumatra *Island* Indonesia 121 B4

Sumba *Island* Indonesia 121 E5

Sumbawanga Tanzania 55 B7

Sumbe Angola 58 B2

Sumgait *see* Sumqayt

Sumqayt Azerbaijan *Rus.* Sumgait 97 H2

Sumy Ukraine 89 F2

Sunderland England, UK 68 D4

Sundsvall Sweden 65 C5

Suntar Russian Federation 94 F3

Sunyani Ghana 53 E4

Superior Wisconsin, USA 20 A1

Superior, Lake *Lake* Canada / USA 15 E3

Suquṭrā *Island* Yemen *var.* Socotra 101 D7 112 B3

Şūr Oman 101 E5

Surabaya Indonesia 120 D5

Sūrat India 114 C5

Surat Thani Thailand 119 C6

Sûre *River* W Europe 67 D7

Surigao Philippines 120 F2

Surinam *see* Suriname 39

Suriname *Country* NE South America *var.* Surinam 39

Surkhob *River* Tajikistan 103 E3

Surt Libya *var.* Sidra 51 G2

Surt, Khalīj *Sea feature* Mediterranean Sea *Eng.* Gulf of Sirte, Gulf of Sidra 51 G2 83 E4

Susanville California, USA 25 B5

Suways, Qanāt as *see* Suez Canal

Suva *Capital of* Fiji 127 E4

Svalbard *External territory* Norway, Arctic Ocean 63 G2

Svay Riêng Cambodia 119 D6

Sverdlovsk *see* Yekaterinburg

Svetlogorsk *see* Svyetlahorsk

Svetozarevo *see* Svyetlahorsk

Svyetlahorsk Belarus *Rus.* Svetlogorsk 87 D7

Swakopmund Namibia 58 B3

Swansea Wales, UK 69 C6

Swaziland *Country* southern Africa 58-59

Sweden *Country* N Europe 64-65

Sweetwater Texas, USA 27 F3

Swindon England, UK 69 D6

Switzerland *Country* C Europe 75

Sydney Australia 130 C3

Sydney Canada 19 G4

Syktyvkar Russian Federation 90 D4 94 C3

Sylhet Bangladesh 115 G4

Syracuse *see* Siracusa

Syracuse New York, USA 21 F3

Syr Darya *River* C Asia 92 C3

Syria *Country* SW Asia 98-99

Syrian Desert *Desert* SW Asia *Ar.* Bādiyat ash Shām 100 A3

Toba, Danau *Lake* Indonesia 120 A3

Toba Kākar Range *Mountains* Pakistan 114 B2

Tobruk *see* Ţubruq

Tocantins *River* Brazil 41 E3

Tocopilla Chile 44 B2

Togo *Country* W Africa 53 F4

Tokat Turkey 96 D3

Tokelau *External territory* New Zealand, Pacific Ocean 122 D3

Tokmak Kyrgyzstan 103 F2

Tokuno-shima *Island* Japan 111 A8

Tokushima Japan 111 B5

Tokyo *Capital of* Japan 111 D5

Toledo Spain 73 E3

Toledo Ohio, USA 20 D3

Toledo Bend Reservoir *Reservoir* S USA 27 H3

Toliara Madagascar 59 F3

Tol'yatti *prev.* Stavropol' Russian Federation 91 C5

Tomakomai Japan 110 D2

Tombouctou Mali 53 E3

Tombua Angola 58 B2

Tomini, Teluk *Sea feature* Indonesia 121 E4

Tomsk Russian Federation 94 D4

Tomur Feng *see* Pobedy

Tonga *Country* Pacific Ocean 122

Tongking, Gulf of *Sea feature* South China Sea *var.* Gulf of Tonkin 109 B7 118 E3

Tongliao China 107 G2

Tongtian He *River* China 106 C4

Tonkin, Gulf of *see* Tongking, Gulf of

Tônlé Sap *Lake* Cambodia 119 D5

Tonopah Nevada, USA 25 C6

Toowoomba Australia 130 C2

Topeka Kansas, USA 23 F4

Torino Italy *Eng.* Turin 76 A2

Tori-shima *Island* Japan 111 D6

Torkestān, Band-e *Mountain range* Afghanistan 102 D4

Torneälv *River* Sweden 64 D3

Tornio Finland 64 D4

Tornio *River* Finland/Sweden 64 D3

Toronto Canada 18 D5

Toros Dağları *Mountain range* Turkey *Eng.* Taurus Mountains 96 C4

Torrens, Lake *Lake* Australia 130 A2

Torreón Mexico 30 D2

Torres Strait *Sea feature* Arafura Sea/Coral Sea 126 B4

Torrington Wyoming, USA 22 D3

Tórshavn *Capital of* Faeroe Islands *Dan.* Thorshavn 63 F4

Tortoise Islands *see* Galapagos Islands

Tortosa Spain 73 F3

Toruń Poland *Ger.* Thorn 78 C3

Toscana *Region* Italy *Eng.* Tuscany 76 B3

Toscano, Archipelago *Island group* Italy 76 A4

Toshkent *see* Tashkent

Tottori Japan 111 B5

Toubkal *Peak* Morocco 48 A2

Touggourt Algeria 51 E2

Toulon France 71 D6

Toulouse France 71 B6

Toungoo Myanmar 118 B4

Tournai Belgium 67 B6

Tours France 70 B4

Townsville Australia 126 B5

Towuti, Danau *Lake* Indonesia 121 E4

Toyama Japan 110 C4

Ţozeur Tunisia 51 E2

Trâblous *see* Tripoli, Lebanon

Trabzon Turkey *Eng.* Trebizond 97 E2

Tralee Ireland 69 A6

Trang Thailand 119 C7

Transantarctic Mountains *Mountain range* Antarctica 132 D3

Transylvania *Region* Romania 88 B3

Transylvanian Alps *see* Carpaţii Meridionali

Trapani Italy 77 C6

Traun Austria 75 D6

Traunsee *Lake* Austria 75 D7

Traverse City Michigan, USA 20 C2

Travis, Lake *Lake* Texas, USA 27 F3

Trebinje Bosnia & Herzegovina 81 C5

Trebizond *see* Trabzon

Trelew Argentina 45 C6

Tremiti, Isole *Island group* Italy 76 D4

Trenčín Slovakia *Ger.* Trentschin *Hung.* Trencsén 79 C6

Trencsén *see* Trenčín

Trento Italy *Ger.* Trient 76 C2

Trenton New Jersey, USA 21 F4

Trentschin *see* Trenčín

Tres Arroyos Argentina 45 D5

Treviso Italy 76 C2

Trient *see* Trento

Trier Germany 75 A5

Trieste Italy 76 D2

Tríkala Greece 82 B4

Trincomalee Sri Lanka 117 E3

Trindade *External territory* Brazil, Atlantic Ocean 47 C6

Trinidad Bolivia 40 C4

Trinidad Uruguay 42 B5

Trinidad *Island* Trinidad & Tobago 36 C1

Trinidad & Tobago *Country* West Indies 35 H5

Trípoli Greece 85 B6

Tripoli Lebanon *var.* Trâblous, Ţarābulus 98 B3

Tripoli *Capital of* Libya *Ar.* Ţarābulus al-Gharb 51 F2

Tristan da Cunha *External territory* UK, Atlantic Ocean 47 D6

Trivandrum India 116 D3

Trnava Slovakia *Ger.* Tyrnau, *Hung.* Nagyszombat 79 C6

Trois-Rivières Canada 19 E4

Trollhättan Sweden 65 B6

Tromsø Norway 64 C2

Trondheim Norway 64 B4

Trondheimsfjorden *Inlet* Norway 64 B4

Troyes France 70 D4

Trujillo Honduras 32 D2

Trujillo Peru 40 A3

Tsarigrad *see* İstanbul

Tschenstochau *see* Częstochowa

Tselinograd *see* Akmola

Tsetserleg Mongolia 106 D2

Tshikapa Zaire 57 C7

Tsumeb Namibia 58 C3

Tsushima *Island* Japan 111 A5

Tubmanburg Liberia 52 C5

Ţubruq Libya *Eng.* Tobruk
51 H2

Tucson Arizona, USA 26 B3

Tucupita Venezuela 39 F4

Tucuruí, Represa de *Reservoir*
Brazil 41 F2

Tudmur Syria *var.* Tadmur,
Eng. Palmyra 98 C3

Tuguegarao Philippines 120 E1

Tuktoyaktuk Canada 12 A2

Tula Russian Federation 91 B5
94 A3

Tulcán Ecuador 38 A4

Tulcea Romania 88 D4

Tulsa Oklahoma, USA 27 G1

Tundzha *River* Bulgaria 84 D2

Tunis *Capital of* Tunisia 51

Tunisia *Country* N Africa 51

Tunja Colombia 38 C2

Tupiza Bolivia 40 C5

Turan Lowland *Lowland*
Turkmenistan/Uzbekistan *var.*
Turan Plain, *Rus.* Turanskaya
Nizmennost' 102 C2

Turan Plain *see* Turan Lowland

Turanskaya Nizmennost' *see*
Turan Lowland

Turčiansky Svätý Martin *see*
Martin

Turin *see* Torino

Turkana, Lake *see* Rudolf, Lake

Turkey *Country* SW Asia 96-97

Turkmenbashy Turkmenistan
prev. Krasnovodsk 102 A2

Turkmenistan *Country* C Asia
102

Turks & Caicos Islands *External
territory* UK, West Indies 35

Turku Finland 65 D6

Turnhout Belgium 67 C5

Turnu Severin *see* Drobeta-
Turnu Severin

Turócszentmárton *see* Martin

Turpan Depression *Lowland*
China 104 B2

Türtkul' Uzbekistan
prev. Petroaleksandrovsk,
Uzb. Türtkül 102 C2

Türtkül *see* Turtkul'

Tuscany *see* Toscana

Tuvalu *Country*
Pacific Ocean 122

Tuxtla Gutiérrez Mexico 31 G5

Tuz Gölü *Lake* Turkey 96 C3

Tuzla Bosnia & Herzegovina
80 C3

Tver' Russian Federation 90 B4

Tweed *River* Scotland, UK
68 D4

Twin Falls Idaho, USA 24 D4

Tyler Texas, USA 27 G3

Tyre *see* Soûr

Tyrnau *see* Trnava

Tyrol *see* Tirol

Tyrrhenian Sea Mediterranean
Sea 77 C6

Tyup Kyrgyzstan 103 G2

U

Ubangi *River* C Africa 57 C5

Uberaba Brazil 41 F5 43 E1

Uberlândia Brazil 41 F5 43 E1

Ubon Ratchathani Thailand
119 D5

Ucayali *River* Peru 40 B3

Uchkuduk Uzbekistan
Uzb. Uchquduq 102 D2

Uchquduq *see* Uchkuduk

Udine Italy 76 C2

Udon Thani Thailand 118 C4

Uele *River* Zaire 56 D5

Ufa Russian Federation 91 D6
94 B3

Uganda *Country* E Africa 55

Uíge Angola 58 B1

Ujungpandang Indonesia
120 E5

Ukmergė Lithuania 86 C4

Ukraine *Country* E Europe 88-89

Ulaanbaatar *see* Ulan Bator

Ulaangom Mongolia 106 C2

Ulan Bator *Capital of* Mongolia
var. Ulaanbaatar 107 E2

Ulan-Ude Russian Federation
95 E4

Uldz *River* Mongolia 107 F1

Ullapool Scotland, UK 68 C3

Ullŭng-do *Island* South Korea
110 B4

Ulm Germany 75 B6

Ulster *Region* Ireland/UK 69 B5

Uluru *Peak* Australia *var.* Ayers
Rock 124 B3

Ul'yanovsk Russian Federation
91 C5

Umanak Greenland 62 B3

Umeå Sweden 64 C4

Umnak Island *Island* Alaska,
USA 16 A3

Una *River* Bosnia &
Herzegovina/Croatia 80 B3

Unalaska Island *Island* Alaska,
USA 16 B3

Ungava, Péninsule d' *Peninsula*
Canada 18 D1

Ungava Bay *Sea feature* Canada
19 E1

United Arab Emirates *Country*
SW Asia 101 D5

United Kingdom *Country*
NW Europe 68-69

United States of America
Country North America 20-29

Uppsala Sweden 65 C6

Ural *River* Kazakhstan/Russian
Federation 91 C7 94 B4

Ural Mountains *Mountain range*
Russian Federation
var. Ural'skiy Khrebet,
Ural'skie Gory 94 C3

Ural'sk Kazakhstan 94 B3

Ural'skiy Khrebet *see* Ural
Mountains

Ural'skie Gory *see* Ural
Mountains

Ura-Tyube Tajikistan 103 E2

Urfa *see* Şanlıurfa

Urganch *see* Urgench

Urgench Uzbekistan *prev.* Novo
Urgench, *Uzb.* Urganch 102 C2

Uroševac Yugoslavia 81 D5

Uruapan Mexico 31 E4

Uruguaiana Brazil 42 B4

Uruguay *Country* SE South
America 42

Uruguay *River* S South America
37 C5

Urumchi *see* Ürümqi

Ürümqi China *prev.* Urumchi

Usa *River* Russian Federation
90 D3

Uşak Turkey *prev.* Ushak 96 B3

Victoria Island *Island* Canada 17 F2

Victoria Land *Region* Antarctica 133 E5

Victoria Nyanza *see* Victoria, Lake

Vidin Bulgaria 84 B1

Viedma Argentina 45 C5

Viekšniai Lithuania 86 B3

Vienna *Capital of* Austria *Ger.* Wien 75 E6

Vientiane *Capital of* Laos 118 C4

Vietnam *Country* SE Asia 118-119

Vigo Spain 72 C2

Vijayawāda India 117 E1

Vila Nova de Gaia Portugal 72 C2

Vila Real Portugal 72 C2

Viliya *see* Neris

Viljandi Estonia *Ger.* Fellin 86 D2

Villach Austria 75 D7

Villahermosa Mexico 31 G4

Villarrica *Peak* Chile 37 B6

Villavicencio Colombia 38 C3

Vilna *see* Vilnius

Vilnius *Capital of* Lithuania *Pol.* Wilno, *Ger.* Wilna, *Rus.* Vilna 87 C5

Viña del Mar Chile 44 B4

Vinh Vietnam 118 D4

Vinnitsa *see* Vinnytsya

Vinnytsya Ukraine *Rus.* Vinnitsa 88 D2

Vinson Massif *Peak* Antarctica 132 B3

Virgin Islands *External territory* USA, West Indies 35 F3

Virginia Minnesota, USA 23 F2

Virginia *State* USA 20-21

Virovitica Croatia 80 B2

Virtsu Estonia *Ger.* Werder 86 C2

Visākhapatnam India 115 E5 117 E1

Visalia California, USA 25 C7

Visby Sweden 65 C7

Viscount Melville Sound *Sea feature* Arctic Ocean 17 F2

Viseu Portugal 72 C3

Vistula *see* Wisła

Vitebsk *see* Vitsyebsk

Viterbo Italy 76 C4

Viti Levu *Island* Fiji 125 F2 127 E4

Vitória Brazil 41 G5 43 G1

Vitoria Spain 73 E1

Vitória da Conquista Brazil 41 G4

Vitória Seamount *Undersea feature* Atlantic Ocean 43 G1

Vitsyebsk Belarus *Rus.* Vitebsk 86 E5

Vjosës, Lumi i *River* Albania 81 D6

Vladikavkaz Russian Federation *prev.* Ordzhonikidze, Dzaudzhikau 91 A7

Vladimir Russian Federation 91 B5

Vladimirovka *see* Yuzhno-Sakhalinsk

Vladivostok Russian Federation 95 G5

Vlieland *Island* Netherlands 66 C1

Vlissingen Netherlands *Eng.* Flushing 67 B5

Vlorë Albania 81 D6

Vojvodina *Region* Yugoslavia 80 D3

Volga *River* Russian Federation 94 A3

Volga Delta *Wetland* Russian Federation 61 G4

Volgograd Russian Federation *prev.* Stalingrad 91 B6 94 A3

Volkovysk *see* Vawkavysk

Vologda Russian Federation 90 B4 94 B2

Vólos Greece 84 B4

Volta, Lake *Lake* Ghana 53 E4

Volta Redonda Brazil 43 E2

Voreioi Sporades *Island group* Greece *Eng.* Northern Sporades 84 C4

Vorkuta Russian Federation 90 E3 94 C2

Vormsi *Island* Estonia *Ger.* Worms, *Swed.* Ormsö 86 C2

Voronezh Russian Federation 91 B5

Võrtsjärv *Lake* Estonia 86 D3

Võru Estonia *Ger.* Werro 86 D3

Vosges *Mountain range* France 70 E4

Vostochno-Sibirskoye More Arctic Ocean *Eng.* East Siberian Sea 12 D2 95 G1

Vostok Island *Island* Kiribati 127 H3

Vrangel'ya, Ostrov *Island* Russian Federation *Eng.* Wrangel Island 12 C1 95 G1

Vratsa Bulgaria 84 C2

Vršac Yugoslavia 80 D3

Vukovar Croatia 80 C3

Vulcano *Island* Italy 77 D6

Vyatka *River* Russian Federation 91 C5

W

Wa Ghana 53 E4

Waag *see* Váh

Waal *River* Netherlands 66 D4

Wabash *River* C USA 20 B4

Waco Texas, USA 27 G3

Waddeneilanden *Island group* Netherlands *Eng.* West Frisian Islands 66 C1

Waddenzee *Sea feature* Netherlands 66 D1

Wadi Halfa Sudan 54 B3

Wad Medani Sudan 54 B4

Wagga Wagga Australia 130 B3

Wagin Australia 129 B6

Waigeo, Pulau *Island* Indonesia 121 G4

Wakayama Japan 111 C5

Wakkanai Japan 110 D1

Wałbrzych Poland *Ger.* Waldenburg 78 B4

Waldenburg *see* Wałbrzych

Wales *National region* UK *Wel.* Cymru 69

Walk *see* Valga

Walla Walla Washington, USA 24 C2

Wallis & Futuna *External territory* France, Pacific Ocean 122 D3

Walvis Bay Namibia 58 B3

Walvis Ridge *Undersea feature* Atlantic Ocean 47 D6

Wandel Sea Arctic Ocean 63 E1

Wanganui New Zealand 131 G3

Wanlaweyn Somalia 55 B6

MAP FINDER

NORTH & WEST ASIA 92

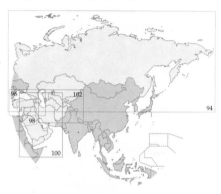

EAST & SOUTH ASIA 104

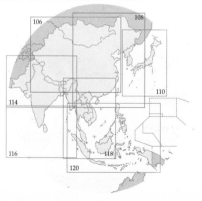